75 QUICK & EASY
BOBBIN LACE PATTERNS

VERONICA SORENSON

B.T. BATSFORD LTD

First published in 1998 by
B.T. Batsford Ltd
9 Blenheim Court
Brewery Road
London N7 9NT
A member of the Chrysalis Group plc

Reprinted 2000

A catalogue record for this book is available from
the British Library.

ISBN 0 7134 8113 7

Printed in Singapore

Designed by DWN Ltd London

DEDICATION
This book is dedicated to my long-suffering and
patient husband, Dennis.

ACKNOWLEDGEMENTS
My thanks are given to all my family, students and
friends for their uncomplaining support, but
especially to my daughter Denise for her skills on
the word processor; Dick Chenery whose
photographic expertise is always gratefully
appreciated; Hazel Holloway for checking the
script; Marilyn Mowatt for her artistic grouping of
lace for photographs; Judy Hemstead and Joan
Underwood for their Honiton interpretations; and
Kathleen Hillyer, Daphne Mullen and Karen
Williams for allowing me to publish their designs.

CONTENTS

INTRODUCTION

The industrial revolution of the 19th century and the invention of machines that made lace quickly and cheaply appeared to eradicate the hand-made lace industry, together with the lacemaker's skills and expertise. However, the dedication and perseverance of a small number of lace schools and lacemakers led to the birth of a new era, in which the art of lacemaking began to emerge as a creative hobby. And now ever-increasing numbers of people are enjoying the click of bobbins between their fingers and the weaving of threads round pins. Indeed, industry has actually contributed to this revival by developing suitable threads in natural fibres, and in a greater range of colours, textures and thicknesses than ever before manufactured.

When lacemaking was their livelihood, lacemakers worked just a few designs in one type of lace. Now that it is a leisure occupation, they are free to enjoy working an unlimited range of techniques. Various lace types may sometimes be combined within one design, with striking effects – even if the 'purist' lacemaker shudders with horror. Modern lace designers have also adapted traditional techniques and created 'new' laces such as Schneeberg and Bruges flower, laces that require fewer bobbins and thicker threads than were used in times gone by. Fortunately, however, traditional techniques such as Honiton, Bucks point and Beds laces have not been lost and are still used in contemporary designs.

This is a book of projects for all those lacemakers who need to make a little gift quickly or who find making a large, complicated piece of lace tedious. The emphasis is on simplicity of technique and the use of a small number of bobbins. This means that the sectional techniques of Bruges flower, Schneeberg, Russian tape and free laces predominate. There are torchon, Honiton and Beds patterns also, but most are not too complex. Nevertheless, there are projects that the advanced lacemaker will enjoy, and many seemingly difficult designs that can be adapted for the real beginner.

There is no 'Techniques' section as such, but there is a list of recommended books on special techniques. Each pattern is star-rated as a guide to indicate the general level of knowledge and ability needed to work the pattern (see Symbolic Notation, page 5).

Modern photocopying machines can enlarge or reduce a design to any size. Many patterns can be simplified by omitting fillings or by mounting on netting. Filling stitches can be altered to achieve a particular effect or to provide a challenge to the more experienced lacemaker. The judicial use of coloured threads can enhance a design, while the colour and texture of backing material can also be used to good effect. Remember that a piece of lace does not have to be complicated or worked in extra fine thread to look beautiful. Often the shape, colour, backing and frame can turn a very simple piece into something quite stunning.

As mentioned above, more than one technique may be incorporated into a design for a special finish. And why not? It is an idea frequently spurned by purists, but put the word 'type' after the lace title (e.g., 'Honiton type') and the adventurer will be absolved from censure!

An indication is given of the number of bobbins required for each project and the thread used. The number of pairs needed for fillings is not given, however, as there is usually room for flexibility here. Needless to say, different threads are available in different countries, and many patterns will be enhanced by using coloured and metallic threads either alone or in combination with white thread. The majority of projects in this book are worked in white simply because black-and-white photographs do not produce clearly defined results. As DMC cotton and BOUC linen threads are available in most countries, many of the designs have been made using these. Note that each thread manufacturer uses different numbering for an equivalent thickness of thread.

If you are unable to find the suggested make of thread, try a small area of cloth stitch in an alternative, using a pricked-out section of your chosen project. If this sample resembles a piece of fabric, that thread will produce good lace. If it is rather open-looking, you need a thicker thread, and if it is too bunched up, with a corrugated effect, you should try a thinner one.

Ideas for new designs come from numerous sources, but it must be remembered that there is 'nothing new under the sun'. Torchon lace designs, for example, are particularly limited in the number of shapes that can be developed, and there is always the risk that two designers working independently and many miles apart might simultaneously arrive at almost identical patterns. I have never consciously plagiarized another designer's work, even if the end results are similar. These things sometimes happen unintentionally, however, and apologies must be made in advance should anyone be distressed that a pattern in this book is similar to one of theirs.

Enjoy making the projects in this book, and I hope you will be inspired to adapt them or perhaps to create your own designs in the future.

Happy lacemaking!

SYMBOLIC NOTATION

All the prickings are shown in the recognized form for that particular type of lace, e.g., Schneeberg-type designs are drawn without pinholes, while Honiton patterns have no working lines. The notation below is used in the prickings and working diagrams.

————	(single line) one pair of bobbins
——	(single thick line) a gimp thread
•	pinhole
✕	Dieppe ground (half-stitch, pin, half-stitch, twist)
⊗	Tulle du Puy (whole stitch, pin, whole stitch)
—/—	one twist
—//—	two twists
—///—	three twists
⬯	tally
☉	hang a pair here to start
✕	lose a pair here to finish
⊗	bead
—o—	picot
══	plait
– – – –	pattern repeat or centre line
✳	star rating – definitely not difficult
✳✳	star rating – some experience needed
✳✳✳	star rating – for the advanced lacemaker

EINLEITUNG

Die industrielle Revolution des 19. Jahrhunderts und die Erfindung von Maschinen, die Spitzen schnell und billig produzierten, schienen die Industrie für handgeklöppelte Spitze einschließlich des Könnens und des Sachverständnisses der Klöpplerinnen völlig zu vernichten. Aber die Hingabe und Ausdauer einer kleinen Anzahl von Klöppelschulen und Klöpplerinnen führte zur Geburt eines neuen Zeitalters, in dem die Kunst des Spitzenklöppelns als eine kreative Freizeitbeschäftigung wiederbelebt wurde. Und nun genießt eine beständig wachsende Zahl von Menschen das Klappern der Klöppel zwischen ihren Fingern und das Weben von Fäden um Nadeln herum.

Manchmal können in einem Muster verschiedene Spitzentechniken, miteinander kombiniert, zu bemerkenswerten Ergebnissen führen – auch wenn die Vertreter der Stilreinheit unter den Klöpplern mit Entsetzen erschauern. Ferner haben moderne Spitzenentwerfer traditionelle Techniken angepaßt und „neue" Spitzen wie Schneeberger Spitze und Brügger Blumenwerk erschaffen; Spitzen, die weniger Klöppel und dickeres Garn erfordern als die vergangener Zeiten. Glücklicherweise aber sind traditionelle Techniken wie Honiton, Bucks Point und Bedford-Spitze nicht verloren gegangen und werden nach wie vor in zeitgenössischen Entwürfen verwendet.

Dieses Buch enthält Entwürfe für alle die Klöpplerinnen, die schnell ein kleines Geschenk brauchen oder die es zu langweilig finden, eine großes, kompliziertes Stück zu arbeiten. Der Schwerpunkt liegt auf Einfachheit der Technik und Verwendung einer kleinen Anzahl von Klöppeln. Das bedeutet, daß zusammengesetzte Spitzen wie Brügger Blumenwerk, Schneeberger, russische Bänderspitze und freie Spitze vorherrschen. Es gibt ebenfalls Torchon-, Honiton- und Bedford-Vorlagen, aber die meisten sind nicht zu kompliziert. Nichtsdestoweniger gibt es Entwürfe, an denen sich fortgeschrittene Klöpplerinnen erfreuen werden und viele, scheinbar schwierige Muster, die für Anfänger vereinfacht werden können.

Es gibt kein „Technik"-Kapitel als solches, aber es gibt eine Liste mit empfehlenswerten Büchern über spezielle Techniken. Jedes Muster ist mit Sternchen bewertet worden, als Hinweis auf das allgemeine Niveau der Kenntnisse und des Könnens, das erforderlich ist, um das Muster arbeiten zu können (Symbolische Bezeichnung, p 7).

Moderne Fotokopierer können ein Muster auf beliebige Maße vergrößern oder verkleinern. Viele Vorlagen können vereinfacht werden durch Weglassen von Füllungen. Füllungen können verändert werden, um eine besondere Wirkung zu erreichen oder um eine Herausforderung für die erfahreneren Klöpplerinnen zu bieten. Der kritische Gebrauch von farbigen Garnen kann einen Entwurf verbessern, obgleich auch Farbe und Struktur des Trägermaterials für eine gute Wirkung eingesetzt werden können. Bedenken Sie, daß eine Spitze nicht kompliziert oder in besonders dünnem Garn gearbeitet sein muß, um wundervoll auszusehen. Oft können Form, Farbe, Träger und Rahmen ein sehr einfaches Stück in etwas ganz Tolles verwandeln.

Es werden Hinweise auf die für jedes Muster erforderliche Anzahl von Klöppeln und das verwendete Garn gegeben. Indessen wird die Anzahl der für die Füllungen benötigten Paare nicht angegeben, da hier normalerweise Platz für Flexibilität ist. Viele Muster gewinnen durch die Verwendung von farbigen und/oder Metallgarnen – entweder allein oder in Verbindung mit weißem Garn. Die Mehrzahl der Entwürfe dieses Buches ist schlicht in weiß geklöppelt, weil Scharzweißfotos keinen entsprechenden Eindruck der Farben bei den Grauabstufungen liefern. Unnötig zu sagen, daß in anderen Ländern andere Garne verfügbar sind. Da DMC-Baumwollgarn und BOUC-Leinengarn in den meisten Ländern verfügbar sind, sind viele Entwürfe mit diesen geklöppelt worden. Beachten Sie, daß jeder Garnhersteller eine unterschiedliche Nummerierung für eine vergleichbare Stärke verwendet.

Wenn Sie außerstande sind, die vorgeschlagene Garnart zu finden, klöppeln Sie mit einer Alternative ein kleines Stück Ihres gewählten Musters, das Sie gestochen haben, im Leinenschlag. Wenn diese Probe einem Stück Stoff ähnelt, liefert das Garn eine gute Spitze. Wenn sie aber ziemlich locker wirkt, brauchen Sie ein dickeres Garn und umgekehrt, wenn sie zu zusammengedrängt ist und sich wellt, sollten Sie ein dünneres Garn wählen.

Ideen für neue Entwürfe kommen aus zahlreichen Quellen, aber es muß daran erinnert werden, daß es „nichts Neues auf der Welt" gibt. Torchonspitzenentwürfe zum Beispiel sind insbesondere in der Anzahl von Mustern, die entwickelt werden können, begrenzt, und es ist immer das Risiko vorhanden, daß zwei Entwerfer, unabhängig voneinander und durch viele Meilen getrennt, gleichzeitig beim Arbeiten zu fast identischen Mustern kommen. Ich habe niemals bewußt die Arbeit anderer Entwerfer nachgeahmt, obwohl es ähnliche Endergebnisse gegeben hat. Diese Dinge passieren manchmal unbeabsichtigt, und so bitte ich bereits im voraus um Entschuldigung, sollte irgend jemand darüber betrübt sein, daß ein Muster in diesem Buch seinem ähnlich ist.

Viel Spaß beim Arbeiten der Muster dieses Buches. Und ich hoffe, daß Sie ermutigt sind, sie an Ihre Vorstellungen anzupassen oder gar für die Zukunft vielleicht Ihre eigenen Klöppelbriefe zu entwerfen.

Also viel Spaß beim Klöppeln!

SYMBOLISCHE BEZEICHNUNG

Alle Klöppelbriefe werden in der für den Spitzentyp charakteristischen Art dargestellt, z.B. Entwürfe in Schneeberger Spitze werden ohne Nadelpunkte gezeichnet, während Honiton-Briefe keine Arbeitslinien haben. Die nachstehend angegebene Bezeichnung wird in den Klöppelbriefen und Arbeitszeichnungen verwendet.

——————	(einzeln Linie) einem Klöppelpaar
——————	(einzeln dicke Linie) einem Konturfaden
•	Nadelpunkt
✕	Dieppe-Grund (Halbschlag-Nadel-Halbschlag-Drehen)
⬯	Tulle du Puy (Leinenschlag-Nadel-Leinenschlag)
——/	ein Dreher
——//	zwei Dreher
——///	drei Dreher
⬭	Formschlag
◉	Hinzufügen eines Paares
✕	Perle
⊗	Herauslegen eines Paares
——o	Pikot
═══	Flechte
– – – –	Rapport oder Symmetrieachse
✳	Klassifizierung durch Sterne - ganz einfach
✳✳	Klassifizierung durch Sterne - einige Kenntnisse erforderlich
✳✳✳	Klassifizierung durch Sterne - für Fortgeschrittene

INLEIDING

De industriâle revolutie in de 19-e eeuw en de uitvinding van machines die snel en vlug kant maakten, bleken funest voor zowel de kantnijverheid als de vakkennis en de bekwaamheid van de kantwerksters. De toewijding en het doorzettingsvermogen van een kleine groep kantwerksters en – scholen leidden echter tot de geboorte van een nieuw tijdperk, waarin de kunst van het maken van kant als creatieve hobby opkwam. En tegenwoordig beleeft een steeds groeiend aantal mensen plezier aan het tikken van de klossen in hun vingers en het weven van draden om spelden.

Verschillende kantsoorten kunnen soms in ÇÇn ontwerp gecombineerd worden met fascinerende effecten – ook al rilt de purist onder de kantwerksters van ontzetting. Moderne kantontwerpers hebben ook traditionele technieken aangepast en "nieuwe" kanten gecreâerd, zoals Schneebergse en Brugs Bloemwerk, kanten waarvoor minder klossen en dikker garen nodig zijn dan vroeger gebruikt werden. Gelukkig zijn de traditionele technieken als Honiton, Bucks point en Bedsfordshire niet verloren gegaan en worden ze in de moderne ontwerpen nog steeds gebruikt.

Dit is een boek met werkstukken voor al die kantklossters, die snel een geschenkje moeten maken of die het maken van een groot, ingewikkeld werk vervelend vinden. De nadruk ligt op de eenvoudige techniek en het gebruik van weinig klossen. Dit betekent dat de technieken van in delen gekloste kanten als Brugs Bloemwerk, Schneeberg, Russische bandkant en de vrije kanten overheersen. Er zijn ook Torchon-, Honiton- en Bedsfordshire-patronen, maar de meeste zijn niet te ingewikkeld. Toch zijn er ook werkstukken waar de gevorderde kantklosster plezier aan zal beleven, naast veel schijnbaar moeilijke tekeningen die aangepast kunnen worden voor de echte beginner.

Er is geen specifiek hoofdstuk "Techniek", maar er is een lijst van aanbevolen boeken over speciale technieken. Elk patroon heeft een steraanduiding die het kennisniveau en de bekwaamheid aangeeft, die nodig zijn voor dat patroon (Symbolische Notatie, p 9).

Moderne kopieermachines kunnen een tekening vergroten of verkleinen tot elk formaat. Veel patronen kunnen vereenvoudigd worden door het weglaten van de vullingen of door ze op tule te naaien. Vullingsslagen kunnen

worden gewijzigd voor een bepaald effect, of om een uitdaging te vormen voor de meer ervaren kantwerkster. Het kritisch gebruik van gekleurde draden kan een ontwerp verfraaien, terwijl kleur en structuur van het achtergrondmateriaal ook gebruikt kunnen worden voor een goed resultaat. Bedenk dat een stuk kant niet ingewikkeld hoeft te zijn of uitgevoerd in extra dun garen om mooi te zijn. Vaak kunnen vorm, kleur, achtergrond en lijst een eenvoudig stuk veranderen in iets magnifieks.

Zoals reeds eerder gezegd, kan voor een speciaal resultaat meer dan ÇÇn techniek gebruikt worden in een ontwerp. En waarom niet? Dit idee wordt door puristen vaak verworpen. Zet echter het woord "type" voor de naam van de kant (bijv. "type Honiton") en iedere avonturier zal gevrijwaard zijn voor kritiek.

Het aantal klossen en het gebruikte garen is voor ieder werkstuk aangegeven. Het aantal paren voor de vullingen is echter niet gegeven, aangezien hier ruimte is voor variatie. Onnodig te zeggen dat in de diverse landen verschillende garens beschikbaar zijn, en dat veel patronen verlevendigd kunnen worden door gekleurde of metallic garens te gebruiken, alleen of in combinatie met wit garen. Het merendeel van de werkstukken in dit boek is geklost in wit om de eenvoudige reden dat zwart-wit foto's geen erg gedetailleerd resultaat geven. Aangezien de DMC katoenen en BOUC linnen garens in de meeste landen verkrijgbaar zijn, zijn deze in veel ontwerpen gebruikt. Houd er rekening mee dat iedere garenfabrikant zijn eigen nummering heeft voor de draaddiktes.

Als u het aangegeven merk garen niet kunt vinden, klos dan een klein stukje in linnenslag in een andere draad, op een uitgeprikt deel van het gekozen werkstuk. Als dit proefstukje lijkt op een stukje geweven stof, zal dat garen een goede kant opleveren. Als het er een beetje los uitziet, hebt u dikker garen nodig, en als het te veel opbolt of plooit, zou u dunner garen moeten proberen.

Uit ontelbare bronnen komen ideeân voor nieuwe ontwerpen. Men moet zich echter realiseren dat "er niets nieuws onder de zon is". Torchonpatronen bijvoorbeeld, zijn bijzonder beperkt in het aantal vormen dat gemaakt kan worden, en er is altijd het risico dat twee ontwerpers onafhankelijk van elkaar en kilometers van elkaar vandaan, tegelijk tot vrijwel gelijke patronen komen. Ik heb nooit bewust andermans werk gebruikt, ook al zijn de resultaten gelijk. Deze dingen gebeuren soms echter onbedoeld en verontschuldigingen worden dan ook bij voorbaat gemaakt, voor het geval iemand pijnlijk getroffen zou zijn doordat een patroon in dit boek lijkt op ÇÇn van de hare.

Veel plezier bij het maken van de werkstukken uit dit boek ! En ik hoop dat u geinspireerd wordt ze aan te passen of misschien in de toekomst uw eigen ontwerpen te creâren.

Veel kantplezier !

SYMBOLISCHE NOTATIE

Alle prikkingen zijn gegeven op de voor die speciale kantsoort erkende manier. Ontwerpen in "Schneebergstijl" zijn bijvoorbeeld getekend zonder speldenpunten, terwijl Honitonpatronen geen werklijnen hebben. De onderstaande notatie is gebruikt in de prikkings en de werktekeningen.

——	een enkele lijn stelt een paar klossen voor
——	een enkele dikke lijn stelt een sierdraadpaar voor speldengat
•	Dieppegrond (netslag, speld, netslag, draaien)

✕	Tulle du Puy (linnenslag, speld, linnenslag)
⊗	ÇÇn keer draaien
—/—	twee keer draaien
—//—	drie keer draaien
—///—	vormslag
⬯	hang hier een paar in om te beginnen
⊙	leg hier een paar uit om te eindigen
✕	kraal
⊗	picot
—o—	vlecht, spijl

═══	steraanduiding - beslist niet moeilijk
– – –	herhaling patroon, of middenlijn
✳	steraanduiding - enige ervaring vereist
✳✳	steraanduiding - voor de gevorderde kantklosster
✳✳✳	Werktekening van de slagen voor de torchonrand

INTRODUCTION

La révolution industrielle du 19ᵉ siècle et l'invention des machines qui peuvent faire rapidement de la dentelle à bon marché a supplanté l'industrie de la dentelle faite à la main, en même temps que le savoir faire et l'expertise. Toutefois, le dévouement et la persévérance d'un petit nombre d'écoles et de dentellières ont permis le renouveau d'une nouvelle ère pour laquelle l'art de denteler commence à émerger en tant que loisir créatif. Et maintenant un nombre croissant de personne s'adonne au cliquetis des fuseaux entre leurs doigts et au va et vient des fils autour des épingles. D'ailleurs l'industrie a bel et bien contribué à ce renouveau en développant les fibres naturelles adéquates, et dans une large palette de coloris, de texture et de finesse, plus qu'il n'en existait auparavant.

Lorsque la dentelle était un revenu, les dentellières ne pratiquaient que peu de modèles dans une même technique. Maintenant, en tant qu'activité de loisirs, elles peuvent aimer s'essayer à toutes sortes de techniques. Parfois on peut réunir plusieurs types de dentelle dans un seul modèle du plus bel effet – même si les "puristes" s'en offusquent. Les dessinateurs de dentelles modernes ont aussi adapté des techniques traditionnelles et créer de

"nouvelles" dentelles comme le Schneeberg et le Fleuri de Bruges, dentelles qui demandent peu de fuseaux et du fil plus gros qu'au temps jadis. Heureusement, cependant, des techniques traditionnelles comme le Honiton, le Bucks et le Beds n'ont pas été oubliées et continuent à être utilisée sur des dessins contemporains.

Voici donc un livre de projets pour les dentellières qui souhaitent faire un petit cadeau vite fait ou qui trouvent qu'un long projet compliqué est fastidieux.

L'accent est mis sur la simplicité de la technique et l'utilisation de très peu de fuseaux. Ceci veut dire qu'on utilisera en partie le Fleuri de Bruges, le Schneeberg, le lacet Russe, la technique libre, en priorité. On trouvera aussi des modèles en Torchon, en Honiton, et en Beds dont la plupart sont assez simples. Mais il y a aussi des modèles que les dentellières plus expérimentées apprécieront et dont certains pourront aussi être adaptés pour des néophytes.

Il n'y a pas de chapitre "techniques" à proprement parlé mais une bibliographie de livres recommandés pour des techniques précises. Un sigle de niveau technique accompagne

chaque modèle pour que chacun puisse faire son choix en fonction de ses connaissances techniques et de son habileté (voir Annotations Symboliques, page 11).

Les nouvelles photocopieuses permettent d'agrandir ou de réduire un modèle à n'importe quelle taille. On peut simplifier un modèle en retirant le fond ou en le cousant sur un tulle. On peut modifier des points d'un fond pour avoir un effet voulu ou par défi pour les plus expérimentées. Le choix judicieux des fils couleurs peut contribuer à la mise en valeur du modèle tout aussi bien que la couleur et la texture du fond support de l'oeuvre. Sachez qu'une pièce de dentelle n'a pas besoin d'être complexe ou faite de fils fins pour être belle. Bien souvent la forme, la couleur, le fond, le cadre, mettront vraiment en valeur un modèle très simple.

Comme indiqué précédemment, on peut utiliser plus d'une technique dans un modèle pour un effet spécial. Et pourquoi pas ? C'est une idée fréquemment méprisée par les puristes, mais ajoutez au nom d'une dentelle le mot "type" (par exemple : "type Honiton") et le téméraire sera absout de toute censure !

Le nombre de fuseaux nécessaires et les fils utilisés sont mentionnés pour chaque modèle. Il n'y a pas cependant d'indication pour les fonds pour vous laissez le libre arbitre. Il ne va pas sans dire que le choix des fils est varié d'un pays à l'autre et qu'on peut utiliser des fils métallisés seuls ou avec du coton blanc. La plupart des modèles de ce livres sont faits en blanc parce que les photos noir et blanc donnent de très bons résultats. Dans la plupart des pays on trouve du coton DMC et du lin BOUC, c'est pourquoi ils sont largement utilisés pour les modèles. Mais faites attention à ce que les différentes manufactures n'attribuent pas le même titrage au même fil.

Au cas ou vous ne pouvez pas utiliser le fil mentionné, faites un échantillon en point toile sur un espace du modèle choisi. Si le résultat donne un bon tissage, ça ira. Si le tissage est trop aéré, choisissez un fil plus gros, et si c'est trop tassé avec un aspect en tôle ondulée, essayez plus fin.

On trouve des idées de nouveaux modèles partout, mais sachez "qu'on ne trouve rien de nouveau sous le soleil". Par exemple, on est vite limité dans le graphisme des modèles en Torchon et il est toujours possible que quelqu'un d'autre sans le savoir et à plusieurs kilomètres de là, fasse en même temps quelque chose de très similaire. Je n'ai jamais voulu copier le travail de quelqu'un d'autre même si le résultat peut y faire penser.

Cela peut arriver sans préméditation et je tiens à m'excuser à l'avance auprès des personnes qui souffriraient de voir des modèles semblables aux leurs dans ce livre.

Ayez plaisir à travailler les modèles proposés dans ce livre et j'espère que vous serez inspiré pour les modifier et pourquoi pas pour faire bientôt vos propres modèles.

Bonne dentelle!

ANNOTATIONS SYMBOLIQUES

Tous les modèles sont tracés selon l'habitude des modèles de leur type, par exemple, en Schneeberg les dessins ne reproduisent pas les trous d'épingle et en Honiton on ne met pas les lignes de travail. Les annotations ci-dessous sont utilisées pour les modèles et pour les diagrammes spécifiques à leur travail.

_____ (seul trait) une paire de fuseaux	•	d'épingle	
_____ (seul trait gras) un fil cordon trou	✕	fond Dieppe (point grille, épingle, point grille, torsion)	
	◉	Tulle du Puy (point toile, épingle, point toile, torsion)	
	/	une torsion	
	//	deux torsions	
	///	trois torsions	
	⬯	point d'esprit mettre une paire ici pour le départ	

⟨◦⟩	Mettre une paire ici pour le départ
✕	rejeter une paire ici pour finir
⊗	perle
──o──	picot
═══	corde de 4
─ ─ ─	motif à répéter ou ligne milieu
✳	vraiment pas difficile
✳✳	un peu d'expérience souhaitée
✳✳✳	pour expertes

CHAPTER ONE
SMALL MOTIFS

KLEINE MOTIVE ✻ KLEINE MOTIEVEN ✻ PETITS MOTIFS

BUTTERFLY *

This is a very simple design, ideal for mounting in a small lid or paperweight.

BOBBINS: 5 pairs for the
body
7 pairs for the
wings
THREAD: DMC Broder
Machine 50

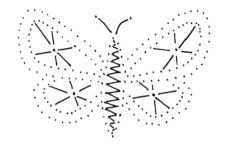

SCHMETTERLING *

Dies ist ein sehr einfaches Muster,
ideal zur Montage in einem
kleinen Deckel oder einem
Briefbeschwerer.

VLINDER *

Dit is een heel eenvoudig
ontwerp, ideaal voor een klein
dekseltje of een presse-papier.

PAPILLONS *

C'est un modèle très simple, idéal
pour un petit couvercle ou un
presse-papiers.

TREBLE CLEF *

This could also be worked using only Honiton lace techniques. The narrow line is made in ten-stick (rib) using 4 pairs. More pairs are added or discarded as needed to work the half-stitch areas.

BOBBINS: 4 pairs for the narrow line more added or discarded for the half-stitch area

THREAD: DMC Broder Machine 50

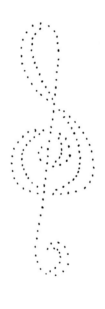

VIOLINSCHLÜSSEL *

Er kann auch ausschließlich in Honitonspitze gearbeitet werden. Die schmale Linie ist als Rippe mit 4 Paaren geklöppelt. Es können in den Halbschlagabschnitten je nach Bedarf mehr Paare hinzugefügt oder hinausgelegt werden.

VIOOLSLEUTEL *

Deze zou ook alleen in Honitontechniek gewerkt kunnen worden. De dunne lijn is gemaakt als een ribje met 4 paar. Meer paren worden voor de netslagdelen in- of uitgelegd waar nodig.

TRIPLE CLEF *

On peut faire ce modèle unique-ment en Honiton. La ligne fine se fait en lacet contour avec 4 paires. On ajoute et rejette plus ou moins de paires en fonction de la section en grille.

BRUGES FLOWER HEART *

The outer braid is decorated with small eyelets, which are worked as shown in the diagram. The flower is worked first, then the braid, and finally the filling.

BOBBINS: 10 pairs for the flower and braid
6 pairs for filling

THREAD: DMC Special Dentelle 80

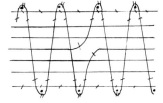

Working method for the eyelet holes

HERZ IN BRÜGGER BLUMENWERK *

Das äußere Band ist mit kleinen Löchern verziert, die laut Zeichnung gearbeitet werden. Zuerst wird die Blüte geklöppelt, dann das Band und zum Schluß die Füllung.

BRUGS BLOEMENHART *

Het buitenste bandje is versierd met kleine openluchtjes, die volgens de werktekening geklost worden. De bloem wordt eerst gewerkt, daarna het bandje en tenslotte de vulling.

COEUR EN FLEURI DE BRUGES *

Le lacet extérieur est décoré d'ajours que l'on fait comme sur le diagramme. On travaille la fleur d'abord, ensuite le lacet, et pour finir le fond.

THE FOUR SEASONS *

A set of coasters, representing spring (daffodil), summer (sunflower), autumn (leaf) and winter (snowflake). The daffodil begins at the base of the trumpet and the stem is worked separately. The sunflower starts with the centre circle. The leaf is commenced at the end of the stem. The snowflake centre is shown in the diagram.

BOBBINS: 5 pairs

THREAD: DMC Broder
Machine 30

Route for the plait filling in
Snowflake

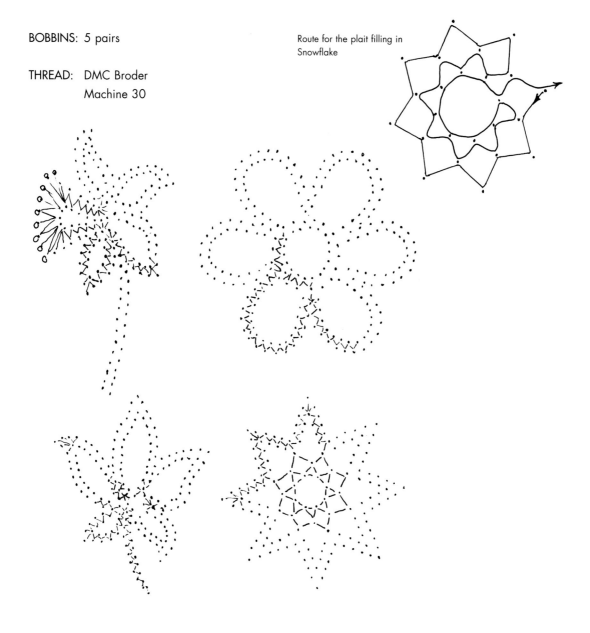

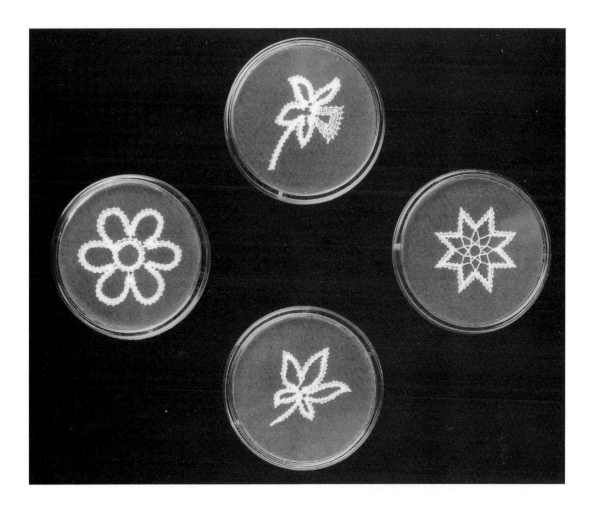

DIE VIER JAHRESZEITEN *

Ein Set von Untersetzern, die Frühling (Narzisse), Sommer (Sonnenblume), Herbst (Blatt) und Winter (Schneeflocke) darstellen. Die Narzisse wird an der Basis des Blütenkelchs begonnen und der Stengel separat gearbeitet. Bei der Sonnenblume wird zuerst der Ring in der Mitte geklöppelt. Beim Blatt beginnt man am Ende des Stengels. Das Schneeflockeninnere ist der Zeichnung zu entnehmen.

DE VIER SEIZOENEN *

Een set onderzetters, die Lente (narcis), Zomer (zonnebloem), Herfst (blad) en Winter (sneeuwvlok) voorstellen. De narcis begint aan de basis van de trompet en de steel is apart gewerkt. De zonnebloem begint bij de middencirkel. Het blad is aan het eind van het steeltje begonnen. Het midden van de sneeuwvlok ziet u in de werktekening.

LES QUATRE SAISONS *

Un set de dessous de verre représente le printemps (jonquille), l'été (tournesol), l'automne (feuille), l'hiver (flocon de neige). Le départ de la jonquille se fait à la base de la trompette et la tige est faite séparément. On commence le tournesol par le cercle du centre.

ANGEL WINGS BOW *

Begin each side at the end of the tail, hanging in the filling pairs as necessary. The fillings are worked at the same time as the braids.

BOBBINS: 5 pairs for each
braid
THREAD: DMC Special
Dentelle 80

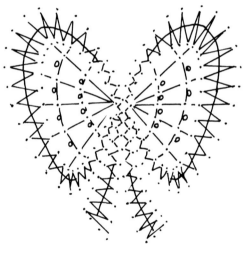

SCHLEIFE *

Begonnen wird jeweils am offenen Schleifenende. Die Paare für die Füllung werden nach Bedarf eingehängt. Die Füllungen werden gleichzeitig mit den Bändern geklöppelt.

STRIK MET ENGELENVLEUGELS *

Begin beide kanten aan het uiteinde van het lint, en hang de paren voor de vulling in waar nodig. De vullingen worden tegelijk met de bandjes geklost.

L'ANGE AUX AILES DÉPLOYÉES *

Commencer chaque côté à chaque extrémité et ajouter les paires des fonds au fur et à mesure. On travaille simultanément les fonds et les lacets.

ENTWINED HEARTS **

The three heart shapes are formed simultaneously, following the order of work shown in the diagram. Sewings are made at the crossings. The original lace was made in three shades of pink.

BOBBINS: 18 pairs   THREAD: DMC Broder
                                    Machine 30

Order of work for Entwined Hearts

VERSCHLUNGENE HERZEN **

Die drei Umrisse der Herzen werden gleichzeitig gemäß der Arbeitsanleitung in der Zeichnung gearbeitet. Angehäkelt wird an den Kreuzungspunkten. Das Original dieser Spitze ist in drei Rosaabstufungen geklöppelt.

INEENGEVLOCHTEN HARTEN **

De drie hartvormen worden tegelijkertijd gemaakt, volgens de in de werktekening aangegeven methode. Bij de kruisingen wordt aangehaakt. De oorspronkelijke kant is in drie tinten rose geklost.

COEURS ENTRELACÉS **

Les trois coeurs se font en même temps et en suivant l'ordre de travail sur le diagramme. Faire des accrochages aux croisements. Le modèle de base est réalisé avec 3 tons de rose.

PRAM **

The pram is worked in Bruges flower techniques. The scrolled spring that joins the wheels is made last. Sewings are made where it crosses and meets the wheels and body. Where it is shown behind the wheels, continue working normally. DO NOT just carry the thread across the back as it will be visible on the right side of the work.

BOBBINS: 6 pairs
THREAD: DMC Cordonnet 60

KINDERWAGEN **

Gearbeitet wurde er im Brügger Blumenwerk. Die verschnörkelte Federung, die die Räder miteinander verbindet, wird zuletzt geklöppelt. Angehäkelt wird, wo sie die Räder kreuzt bzw. das Wagenoberteil und die Räder berührt. An den verdeckten Kreuzungspunkten wird normal weitergeklöppelt. NICHT nur die Paare hinten weiterführen, weil es auf der rechten Seite der Arbeit sichtbar ist.

KINDERWAGEN **

De kinderwagen is in de Brugs Bloemwerk techniek gewerkt. De gekrulde veer die de wielen verbindt, wordt het laatst gemaakt. Waar hij de wielen en de bak kruist of raakt wordt aangehaakt. Waar hij achter de wielen te zien is moet u op de normale manier doorwerken. Voer de draden NIET alleen maar door langs de achterkant, aangezien dit aan de goede kant van het werk zichtbaar is.

LANDAU **

Le landau est fait en Fleuri de Bruges. On fait en dernier la volute des amortisseurs qui joignent les roues. Faire des accrochages aux points de croisement et quand les roues touchent la caisse. Quand vous voyez derrière les roues, continuez normalement le travail. NE PAS faire traverser les fils derrière parce que ça se voit sur l'endroit.

FOUNTAIN **

Here is another design that uses Bruges flower techniques. Each plume of water starts at the base in cloth stitch and gradually changes to half-stitch as it reaches the top, concluding with a Bruges scroll.

BOBBINS: the number of pairs is left to your own judgement

THREAD: DMC Broder Machine 30

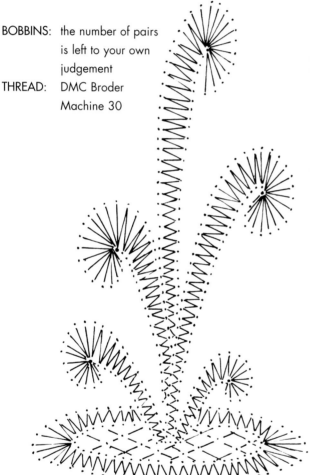

SPRINGBRUNNEN **

Hier ist ein weiterer Entwurf, der Elemente des Brügger Blumenwerks verwendet. Jeder Wasserstrahl beginnt an der Basis im Leinenschlag und wechselt nach oben hin allmählich zum Halbschlag.

FONTEIN **

Dit is nog een ontwerp volgens de techniek van het Brugs Bloemwerk. Iedere waterstraal start aan de basis in linnenslag en gaat van lieverlede over in netslag tot de top, waar hij in een Brugse krul eindigt.

FONTAINE **

Voici un autre dessin en Fleuri de Bruges. Chaque jet d'eau commence par le bas en point toile et change peu à peu en grille vers le haut pour se terminer en volute.

TOADSTOOLS ***

The fillings have been shown diagrammatically as a pricking might be confusing. The tops are worked with half-stitch spots and plaits. The central stem is worked in honeycomb ground, and the other two stems are in Tulle du Puy and rose ground.

BOBBINS: 6 pairs for the
                 mound
                 3 pairs for the
                 braids
THREAD: BOUC fil de lin 100

PILZE ***

Die Füllungen werden schematisch dargestellt, da ein Pricking hier verwirrend sein könnte. Bei den Pilzköpfen werden Halbschlagflecken mit Flechtern verbunden. Der mittlere Stiel ist im Rosengrund geklöppelt worden und die beiden anderen in Leinenschlag - Nadel Leinenschlag (Tulle du Puy) Rohrstuhlgrund.

PADDESTOELEN ***

De vullingen zijn hier als werktekening gegeven, omdat een prikking misschien verwarrend zou kunnen zijn. De hoeden zijn geklost met netslagvlekken en spijlen. De middelste steel is in Rozengrond geklost, en de andere twee stelen in "Tulle du Puy" en Vierge.

CHAMPIGNONS ***

Voir les fonds sur le diagramme, ils seraient trop confus sur le modèle. Sur les chapeaux faire des pois en grille et des cordes de quatre. La queue au centre est en point vitré, les deux autres en Tulle du Puy et fond mariage.

IRISES ***

The original lace has lemon-yellow flowers and green leaves, worked in a free lace style. It can also be made using Honiton techniques (you may want to reduce the size). The diagram shows the order and direction of work.

BOBBINS: depends on method
of construction and
threads used

THREAD: DMC Broder
Machine 30

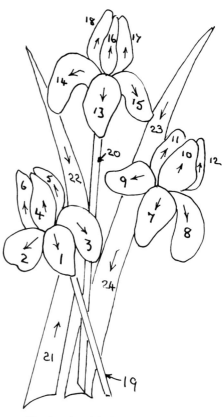

Direction of work for Irises

SCHWERTLILIE ***

Die Originalspitze hat
zitronengelbe Blüten und grüne
Blätter in „freier" Spitzen-Technik.
Sie könnte ebenso mit Honiton-
Techniken gearbeitet werden
(dazu empfiehlt es sich, die Größe
zu reduzieren). Die Zeichnung
zeigt die Reihenfolge und
Richtung der Arbeit.

IRISSEN ***

De originele kant heelt
citroengele bloemen en groene
bladeren, als vrije kant gewerkt.
Hij kan ook volgens de
Honitontechniek geklost worden.
(Dan wilt u misschien het formaat
verkleinen). De werktekening
geeft volgorde en werkrichting
aan.

IRIS ***

Sur le modèle de base les fleurs
sont jaune citron avec des feuilles
vertes. On peut aussi les faire en
Honiton (il faut alors réduire la
taille). Suivre le diagramme pour
l'ordre et la direction du travail.

CHAPTER TWO
CHRISTMAS LACE

WEIHNACHTLICHE SPITZE ✳ KANT VOOR KERSTMIS
✳ MOTIFS DE NOËL

SMALL CHRISTMAS TREE *

Start the outline braid at any suitable point. The decorative honeycomb filling is worked half-stitch, twist, pin, half-stitch, twist at each pin. Pairs are hung in and discarded as necessary.

BOBBINS: 6 pairs for the edge braid

THREAD: DMC Broder Machine 30

KLEINER WEIHNACHTSBAUM *

Beginnen Sie mit dem Umrißband an einer beliebigen geeigneten Stelle. Die dekorative Rosengrundfüllung wird an jeder Nadel Halbschlag - Drehen - Nadel - Halbschlag - Drehen geklöppelt. Nach Bedarf werden Paare eingehängt oder hinausgelegt.

KLEINE KERSTBOOM *

Begin het bandje voor de omtrek op een geschikte plaats. De decoratieve Rozengrond is op iedere speld als volgt geklost: netslag, draaien, speld, netslag, draaien. Waar nodig, worden paren in- of uitgehangen.

PETIT SAPIN DE NOËL *

Commencer par le contour en lacet sur un endroit approprié. Le fond en point vitré se fait en point grille, torsion, épingle, point grille torsion sur chaque épingle. On ajoute et rejette les paires là où il faut.

LARGE CHRISTMAS TREE *

Start at the base of the trunk and work in a zig-zag fashion up one side and down the other, making sewings at the centre. The beads are added as shown in the diagram.

BOBBINS: 4 pairs
THREAD: DMC Broder
         Machine 30

14 small beads

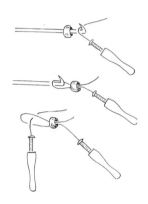

Adding beads

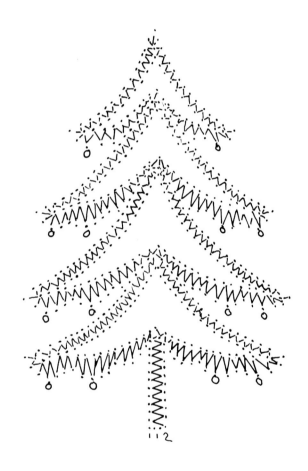

GROSSER WEIHNACHTSBAUM *

Beginnen Sie am Fuß des Stammes und arbeiten Sie im Zickzack die eine Seite hinauf und die andere hinunter, wobei Sie jeweils in der Mitte einhäkeln. Die Perlen werden wie in der Zeichnung angegeben eingefügt.

GROTE KERSTBOOM *

Begin onderaan de stam en werk zigzagsgewijs langs ÇÇn kant omhoog en langs de andere kant weer naar beneden, terwijl u in het midden aanhaakt. De kralen worden volgens de werktekening gebruikt.

GRAND SAPIN DE NOËL *

Commencer à la base du tronc et monter une moitié en zigzag et redescendre l'autre par accrochages au centre. Pour les ajouts de perles, suivre le diagramme.

THREE LITTLE STARS *

Each star requires only 2 pairs of bobbins. They are worked following the route shown in the diagram in the manner of Russian tape lace fillings.

BOBBINS: 2 pairs
THREAD: DMC Special
Dentelle 80

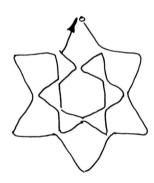

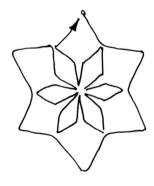

Route taken for the fillings in the Little Stars

2

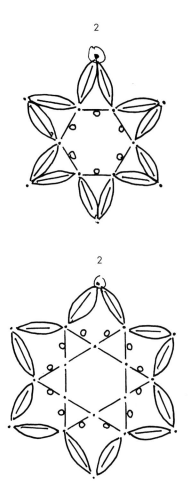

2

2

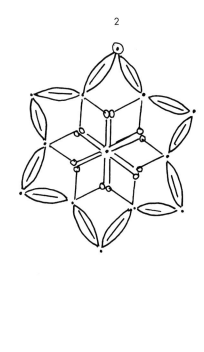

DREI KLEINE STERNE *

Jeder Stern erfordert nur 2 Klöppelpaare. Gearbeitet wird gemäß dem in der Zeichnung dargestellten Verlauf nach Art und Weise der Füllungen der russischen Bänderspitze.

DRIE STERRETJES *

Voor elke ster zijn niet meer dan 2 paar klossen nodig. Ze zijn geklost als vullingen in Russische bandkant, volgens de in de werktekening aangegeven route.

TROIS PETITES ETOILES *

Prendre seulement 2 paires de fuseaux pour chaque étoile. Le cheminement du travail suit la technique des fonds Russes.

TWO HANGING STARS *

The plaited edge (as worked in Schneeberg lace) in this pattern gives the stars strength. The narrow cloth-stitch areas are decorated with silver and gold 'glitter glue'.

BOBBINS: 8 pairs
THREAD: DMC Special
Dentelle 80

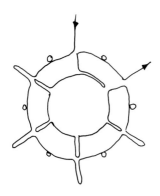

The centre detail for the second Hanging Star

ZWEI SCHWEBENDE STERNE *

Der Flechterrand (gearbeitet wie bei der Schneeberger Spitze) in diesem Klöppelbrief gibt den Sternen Halt. Die engen Leinenschlag-Bereiche sind mit silbernem und goldenem „Glitzerkleber" verziert.

TWEE HANGENDE STERREN *

De gevlochten rand (als in Schneebergse Kant) in dit patroon geeft de sterren stevigheid. De smalle linnenslagdelen zijn versierd met zilveren en gouden "glitterlijm".

DEUX ETOILES À SUSPENDRE *

Faire un bord en corde (façon Schneeberg) pour renforcer la bordure des étoiles. Les petites parties toilées sont décorées de "glitter glue" or et argent.

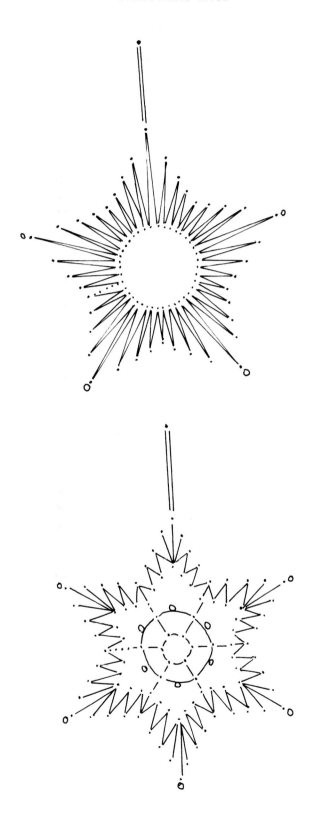

BEADED STAR **

The order of working for the plaited filling is shown in the diagram. The lace has been mounted in a powder compact.

Edge
BOBBINS: 6 pairs
THREAD: DMC Broder
          Machine 30

Filling
BOBBINS: 2 pairs
THREAD: DMC Special
          Dentelle 80

16 seed beads

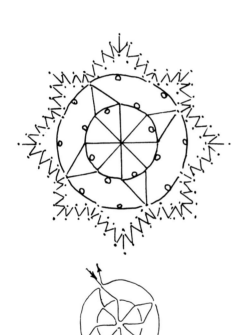

Route for the centre plait of the Beaded Star

PERLENBESETZTER STERN **

Die Reihenfolge, wie die Füllung aus Flechten zu klöppeln ist, wird in der Zeichnung angegeben. Die Spitze ziert eine Puderdose.

STER MET KRALEN **

De werkvolgorde voor de spijlenvulling vindt u in de werktekening. De kant is in een poederdoos gemonteerd.

ETOILE PERLÉE **

Suivre le diagramme pour l'ordre du travail du fond en cordes. La dentelle est présentée sur un poudrier.

BELL *

The braid begins at the top with 6 pairs. For the half-stitch area, 2 extra pairs are added which are discarded when the braid reverts to whole stitch. A large pearl bead is used for the clapper. The diagram shows the route taken for the filling.

BOBBINS: 8 pairs
THREAD: DMC Broder
Machine 30

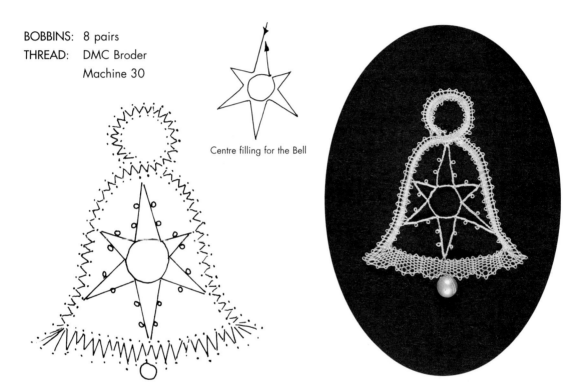

Centre filling for the Bell

GLOCKE *

Das Band beginnt oben am Glockenscheitel mit 6 Paaren. Für den Halbschlagabschnitt werden 2 zusätzliche Paare benötigt, die wieder herausgenommen werden, wenn das Band zum Leinenschlag zurückwechselt. Für den Klöppel wird eine große Perle verwendet. Die Skizze zeigt den Verlauf, nach dem die Füllung zu klöppeln ist.

KLOK *

Het bandje begint bovenaan met 6 paar. Voor het netslagdeel worden 2 extra paren bijgehangen, die weer uitgelegd worden waar het bandje weer in linnenslag overgaat. Een grote kraal vormt de klepel. De werktekening geeft de route voor de vulling aan.

CLOCHE *

Commencer le lacet en haut avec 6 paires. Pour la zone en grille, ajouter 2 paires qui seront rejetées quand la grille change en point toile. Mettre une grosse perle sur le battant. Suivre le diagramme pour le cheminement du fond.

ANGEL **

This little angel is worked using Schneeberg lace techniques. She is made in one continuous braid, with simultaneous fillings.

BOBBINS: 12 pairs
THREADS: DMC Special
Dentelle 80

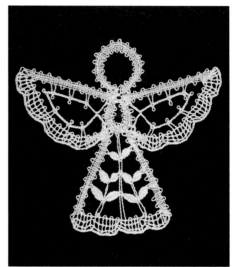

ENGEL **

Bei diesem kleinen Engel werden Elemente der Schneeberger Spitze verwendet. Er wird aus einem fortlaufenden Band geklöppelt. Die Füllungen werden gleichzeitig mitgearbeitet.

ENGEL **

Dit engeltje is volgens de Schneebergtechniek geklost. Ze is gemaakt als een doorlopende band, terwijl de vullingen tegelijkertijd geklost zijn.

ANGE **

Ce petit ange reprend la technique Schneeberg. C'est un lacet en continu avec des variations de fonds.

CANDLE **

This colourful design is made in Bruges flower lace. The various components are made in the following order: candle, leaves, flame, ribbon.

BOBBINS: 7 pairs for the
candle
5 pairs for the
leaves
6 pairs for the flame
5 pairs for the
ribbon

THREAD: DMC Special
Dentelle 80

KERZE **

Dieser farbenprächtige Entwurf ist im Brügger Blumenwerk entstanden. Die verschiedenen Komponenten werden in folgender Reihenfolge gearbeitet: Kerze, Blätter, Flamme, Band.

KAARS **

Dit kleurige ontwerp is als Brugs Bloemwerk geklost. De verschillende onderdelen zijn in deze volgorde gemaakt: kaars, bladeren, vlam, strik.

BOUGIE **

Ce modèle très coloré est fait en Fleuri de Bruges. Les éléments qui la composent sont faits dans l'ordre suivant: bougie, feuilles, flamme, ruban.

CHAPTER THREE
ANIMAL KINGDOM

DAS TIERREICH ❋ HET KONINKRIJK DER DIEREN
❋ BESTIAIRE

'SOOTY' CAT *

Use this lucky black cat motif on a child's article of clothing or make a picture of it. It is worked in Schneeberg techniques, starting from the tail.

BOBBINS: 7 pairs
THREAD: DMC Special
Dentelle 80

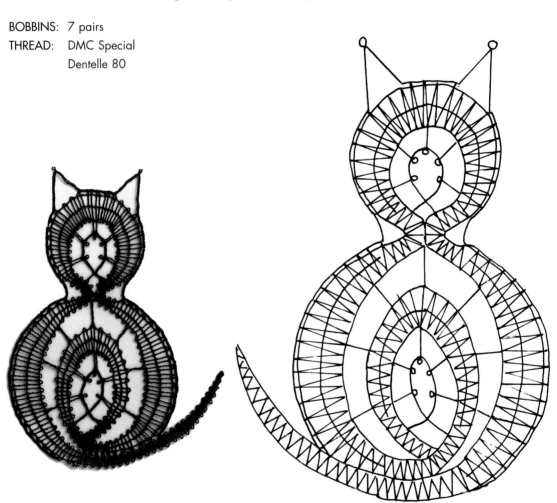

„SCHWARZE" KATZE *

Diese hübsche schwarze Katze eignet sich als Applikation auf Kinderkleidung oder als Bild. Sie wird, am Schwanz beginnend, in Schneeberger Technik geklöppelt.

POES "ROETJE "*

Gebruik dit (Engelse) geluksmotief van een zwarte kat op kinderkleding of maak er een schilderijtje van. Het is volgens de Schneebergtechniek gewerkt, te beginnen bij de staart.

LE CHAT "SOOTY "*

Voici un motif à coudre sur un vêtement d'enfant ou en faire un petit tableau. On le fait en Schneeberg en commençant par la queue.

DINOSAURS *

These two little designs are worked in ten-stick (rib), with no fillings. They are ideal for sewing on to children's clothing or they could be enlarged with fillings to make a picture.

BOBBINS: 6 pairs
THREAD: DMC Broder
Machine 50

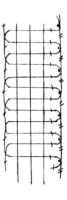

Adaptation of the 'rib' or 'ten-stick' for the Dinosaurs using fewer twists

DINOSAURIER *

Diese zwei kleinen Saurier werden als Rippe (Honiton) geklöppelt - ohne Füllungen. Sie sind ideal, um sie auf Kinderkleidung zu nähen oder um sie zu vergrößern und mit Füllungen als Bild zu arbeiten.

DINOSAURUS *

Deze twee ontwerpjes zijn als een ribje geklost, zonder vulling. Ze zijn ideaal om op kinderkleding te naaien of ze zouden vergroot kunnen worden voor een schilderijtje.

DINOSAURES *

Ces deux petits motifs sont faits en lacet contour sans fond. Ils peuvent être facilement cousus sur des vêtements d'enfant ou on peut les agrandir et y ajouter des fonds pour en faire un tableau.

LARGE BUTTERFLY *

Here is a simple tape lace butterfly. The front edge of the wings has a straight edge (no extra pairs). The filling is in the style of Beds lace and is worked as shown in the diagram. It looks beautiful made in multi-coloured thread.

BOBBINS: 5 pairs for the braid
THREAD: DMC Special
Dentelle 80

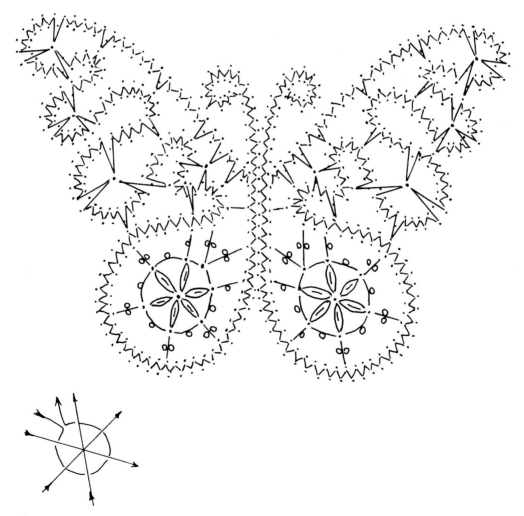

Route for the filling pairs of the Butterfly

GROSSER SCHMETTERLING *

Der Schmetterling besteht aus einer einfachen Bänderspitze. Die Flügelvorderkante hat einen glatten Rand (Innenrand) (keine zusätzlichen Paare). Die Füllung ist im Stil der Bedford-Spitze und wird wie in der Zeichnung angegeben gearbeitet. Er sieht wunderschön mit farbverlaufendem Garn geklöppelt aus.

GROTE VLINDER *

Dit is een eenvoudige vlinder in bandkant. De voorkant van de vleugels heeft een rechte buitenrand (geen extra paren). De vulling is in de stijl van de Bedsfordshire kant en is volgens de werktekening geklost. In veelkleurig garen ziet hij er schitterend uit.

GRAND PAPILLON *

C'est tout simplement un papillon en lacet. Faire un bord droit (sans ajouter de paires) pour les ailes. Faire les fonds façon Beds en suivant le diagramme. C'est très joli en fil nuancé.

'SAMMY' SNAIL *

This is another little Schneeberg motif. The start and finish point is the rear base of the shell.

BOBBINS: 6 pairs
THREAD: DMC Special
Dentelle 80

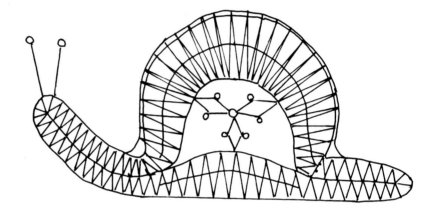

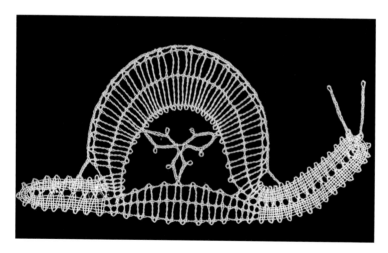

SCHNECKE „SAMMY" *

Ein weiteres kleines Schneeberger Motiv. Der Anfangs- und Endpunkt ist das hintere Ende des Schneckenhauses.

"SAMMY" DE SLAK *

Dit is nog een Schneebergmotiefje. Begin en eind liggen onderaan de achterkant van het slakkenhuis.

L'ESCARGOT "SAMMY "*

Encore un autre motif en Schneeberg. Le départ et l'arrivée sont à l'arrière de la base de la coquille.

MUMMY BEAR *

Work tallies for the eyes and snout area in black first, then join the edge braid to these with sewings. The filling is Tulle du Puy.

BOBBINS: 5 pairs for the
          outline
THREAD: DMC Broder
          Machine 30

MAMA BÄR *

Zuerst arbeiten Sie Formschläge in schwarz für die Augen und die Schnauze. Dann verbinden Sie diese mit dem Konturband. Die Füllung wird Leinenschlag - Nadel - Leinenschlag (Tulle du Puy) geklöppelt.

MAMA BEER *

Klos eerst de blaadjes voor de ogen en de snuit in zwart, verbind dan het bandje hiermee door aanhakingen. De vulling is "Tulle du Puy".

MAMAN OURS *

Faire d'abord des points d'esprit pour les yeux et le museau noir, ensuite raccorder ces parties au bord en lacet par des accrochages. Utiliser le fond Tulle du Puy.

ANIMAL KINGDOM

Both prickings have been reproduced at
80%. Please enlarge on a photocopier
by 125% for actual size

BABY BEAR AND BALL *

Work the eyes and snout in black first, like Mummy Bear. The rest of the bear is brown, except for the hand and foot fillings, which are black.

The ball is worked in half-stitch, starting with 8 pairs and increasing to 11 pairs. Add or lose the extra pairs at the inner edge. The inner edge pins are worked more than once, using the lines on the pricking as a guide.

Baby bear
BOBBINS: Outline 5 pairs
THREAD: DMC Broder
Machine 30

Ball
BOBBINS: 8 pairs, increasing
to 11
THREAD: DMC Broder
Machine 30

BABY BÄR MIT BALL *

Als erstes werden, wie bei Mama Bär, die Augen und Schnauze in schwarz geklöppelt. Der Rest des Bären ist, bis auf die Füllungen der Hand und des Fußes, die auch schwarz sind, braun.
Der Ball wird im Halbschlag gearbeitet und mit acht Paaren begonnen. Die Anzahl der Paare erhöht sich bis auf 11. Die zusätzlichen Paare werden am Innenrand hereingenommen bzw. hinausgelegt.

BABY BEER MET BAL*

Klos eerst de ogen en de snuit in zwart, als bij Mama Beer. De rest van de beer is bruin, behalve de vullingen in handen en voeten, die weer zwart zijn.
De bal is in netslag geklost, beginnend met 8 paar en verbredend tot 11 paar. Leg deze paren aan de binnenkant in of uit. De spelden op de binnenrand worden meermalen gebruikt. Neem de lijnen op de prikking als leidraad.

BÉBÉ OURSON ET BALLE*

Commencer par les yeux et le museau noir comme pour la Maman Ours. Faire le reste en marron, sauf pour les paumes et plantes de pieds qui sont en noir. Faire la balle en grille, en commençent avec 8 paires qu'on augmente jusqu'à 11 paires. Les ajouts et rejets se font sur le bord intérieur. On utilise plusieurs fois les mêmes épingles du bord intérieur, suivre les lignes du modèle comme guide.

'TOMMY' TORTOISE **

Designed by Karen Williams, this pattern can be enlarged or reduced as the line drawing shows. Two interpretations of the smaller version, by Judy Hempstead and Joan Underwood, are also shown. The fillings can be altered as required.

BOBBINS: Depends on method of construction and threads used

THREAD: DMC Broder Machine 50 for the larger version 180 Honiton thread for the smaller version

SCHILDKRÖTE „TOMMY" **

Dieser Klöppelbrief, entworfen von Karen Williams, kann vergrößert oder verkleinert werden. Zwei Interpretationen der kleineren Version von Judy Hemstead und Joan Underwood werden ebenfalls abgebildet. Die Füllungen können nach Belieben geändert werden.

"TOMMY" SCHILDPAD **

Dit, door Karen Williams ontworpen, patroon kan zoals de tekening laat zien, worden vergroot of verkleind. Twee, door Judy Hemstead en Joan Underwood uitgevoerde, kleine versies zijn ook afgebeeld. De vullingen kunnen naar believen worden gewijzigd.

"TOMMY" LA TORTUE **

Ce dessin est fait par Karen Williams, et ce modèle peut être agrandis ou réduits comme le montrent les lignes du dessin. On peut voir deux versions du petit modèle interpretées par Judy Hemstead et par Joan Underwood. Au besoin, modifier les fonds.

'KANGA' AND 'ROO' **

Remember that the part of the pattern that would be closest to you if it was 3D must be worked first. Straight lines represent 'rib'; the photograph shows suggested filling stitches.

BOBBINS: Up to 6 pairs for the outline
THREAD: DMC Broder Machine 30

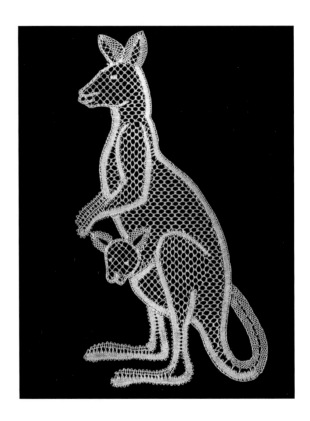

„KANGA" UND „ROO" **
(KÄNGURUHS)

Denken Sie daran, daß der Teil des Klöppelbriefes, der Ihnen am nächsten wäre, wenn es 3D wäre, zuerst geklöppelt werden muß. Gerade Linien kennzeichnen eine Rippe. Die Fotografie zeigt mögliche Gründe als Füllung.

"KANGA" EN "ROE" **

Denk eraan dat het deel van het patroon dat in een 3-D uitvoering het dichtst bij u zou zijn, het eerst moet worden gewerkt. Strakke lijnen stellen een ribje voor; de foto geeft suggesties voor de vullingen.

"KANGA" ET "ROO" **

Faire attention à ce que la partie qui serait la plus proche de vous si c'était de la 3D doit être travaillée d'abord. Un trait droit veut dire "lacet contour"; la photo propose certains fonds.

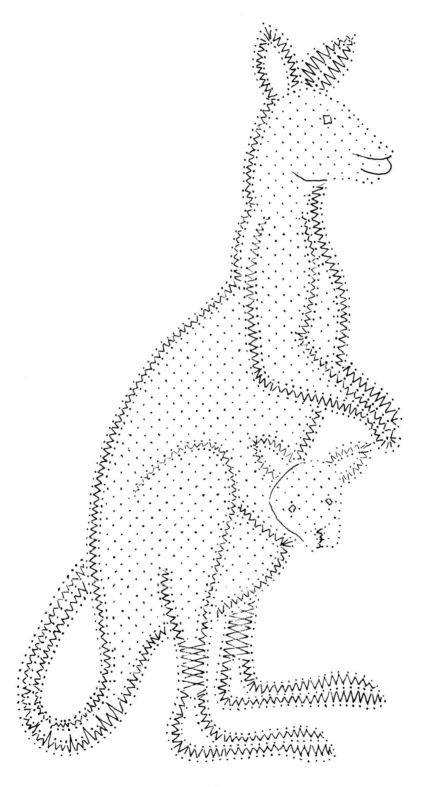

WELSH DRAGON ***

This design is complicated, but is included at the request of many lacemakers. It is reproduced here at 80 per cent of the original size. The change from honeycomb to triangular ground at the base of the wing is shown in the diagram as there is no break in the pricking. The dragon is worked in scarlet.

BOBBINS: depends on method of construction and threads used

THREAD: DMC Broder Machine 30

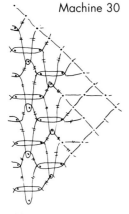

Welsh Dragon – changing from honeycomb to triangular ground

WALISISCHER DRACHE ***

Dieser Entwurf ist kompliziert, aber er wurde aufgrund der Nachfrage vieler Klöpplerinnen ins Buch aufgenommen. Der Klöppelbrief wird hier auf 80 % verkleinert gegenüber dem Original wiedergegeben. Der Wechsel vom Rosengrund zum Pagodengrund am Flügelansatz ist hier dargestellt, als ob keine Unterbrechung im Pricking ist. Der Drache ist in scharlachrotem Garn geklöppelt.

DRAAK UIT WALES ***

Dit is een ingewikkeld ontwerp, echter opgenomen op verzoek van vele klossters. Het is hier afgebeeld op 80% van de ware grootte. Omdat er geen onderbreking is in de prikking, wordt de overgang van Rozengrond naar Driehoeksgrond aan de basis van de vleugel aangegeven. De draak is in scharlakenrood uitgevoerd.

DRAGON GALLOIS ***

Ce dessin est complexe, mais il est ajouté à la demande de beaucoup de dentellières. Il est reproduit ici à 80% de la taille réelle. Bien regarder l'évolution du point vitré en point triangle à la base des ailes parce qu'il n'y a pas de changement sur le dessin. Le dragon se fait en rouge.

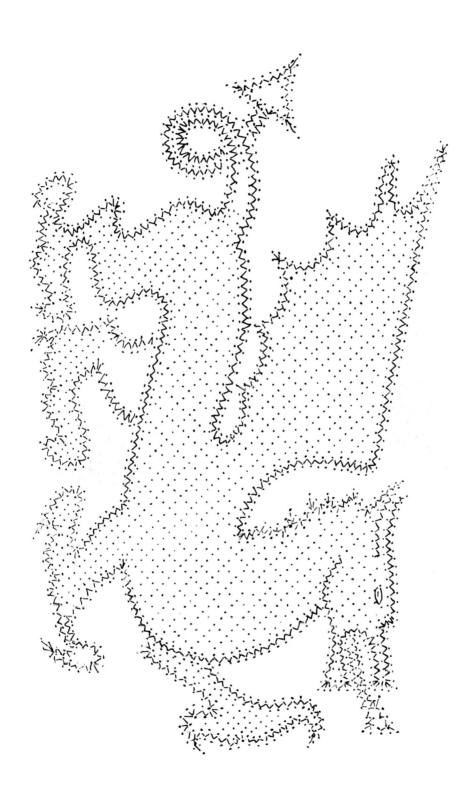

CHAPTER FOUR
MAT EDGINGS

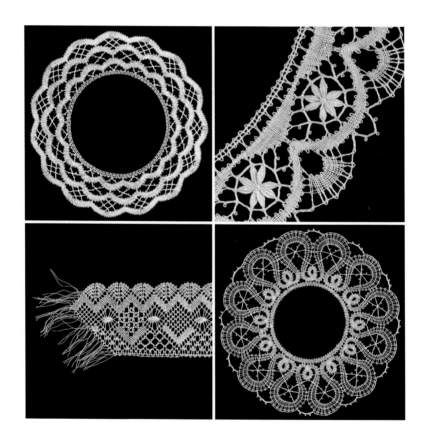

SPITZEN RANDER FUR DECKCHEN ✳ RANDEN VOOR
KLEEDJES ✳ BORDURES POUR SETS DE TABLE

TORCHON EDGE ***

This extremely versatile design can be interpreted in a number of ways – a square, a rectangle, a small circle requiring 9 pattern repeats to complete the ring, and a large circle that needs 18 repeats.

The versatility of torchon lace means that different stitches can be worked using the same pricking. The sample illustrates some of these, but the lacemaker can experiment for herself.

BOBBINS: 30 pairs
THREAD: DMC Cordonnet 80

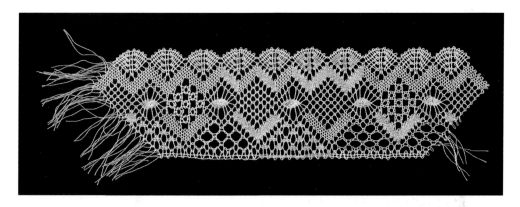

TORCHON-RAND ***

Dieses sehr vielseitige Muster kann auf verschiedene Weise verwendet werden - als Quadrat, als Rechteck, als kleiner Kreis mit 9 Musterblöcken oder als großer mit 18 Rapports für einen kompletten Ring.
Die Vielseitigkeit von Torchonspitze bedeutet, daß verschiedene Schläge auf demselben Klöppelbrief geklöppelt werden können. Die Abbildung zeigt einige Varianten, aber jeder für sich kann weitere ausprobieren.

TORCHONRAND ***

Dit bijzonder veelzijdige ontwerp kan op een aantal manieren worden uitgevoerd - een vierkant, een rechthoek, een kleine cirkel van 9 rapporten en een grote cirkel van 18 rapporten.
De veelzijdigheid van torchonkant bestaat hierin dat op ÇÇn prikking verschillende slagen kunnen worden gebruikt. Het voorbeeld laat er enkele van zien, maar de kantklosster kan ook zelf experimenteren.

BORDURE TORCHON ***

Voici un modèle qui peut avoir de multiples interprétations- un carré, un rectangle, un petit rond pour lequel on fera 9 répétitions pour le rond complet et un plus grand qui en demande 18.
Les différentes interprétations du Torchon se travaillent sur le même dessin.
On peut en voir un échantillonnage mais la dentellière peut essayer à son gré.

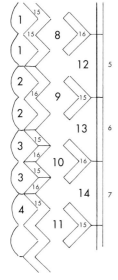

Different stitches on the
Torchon Edge sampler

Head

area 1   whole stitch and twist
both pairs

area 2   whole stitch both pairs

area 3   whole stitch worker and
whole stitch and twist
passives

area 4   whole stitch and twist
worker and whole stitch
passives

Foot

area 5   whole stitch and twist all
pairs

area 6   whole stitch passives
and whole stitch and
twist worker

area 7   straight edge; all pairs
whole stitch and twist

Grounds

area 8   half-stitch rose ground

area 9   Dieppe ground (half-
stitch, pin, half-stitch,
twist)

area 10   Tulle du Puy (whole
stitch, pin, whole stitch,
twist)

area 11   whole stitch rose ground

area 12   honeycomb (half-stitch,
twist, pin, half-stitch,
twist)

area 13   triangular ground

area 14   honeycomb (whole
stitch, twist, pin, whole
stitch, twist)

Trails

area 15   half-stitch

area 16   whole stitch

FESTOONS *

A circular design in the style of Beds lace, this is worked in an anti-clockwise direction. The outer trail carries the filling pairs along where necessary, while the pairs for the inner trails are taken across the outer trail as shown in the diagram. Fifteen repeats of the pattern complete the ring.

BOBBINS: 28 pairs
THREAD: BOUC Fil de Lin 80

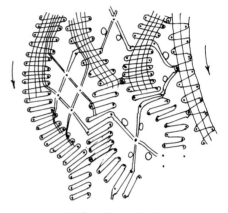

Working diagram for Festoons

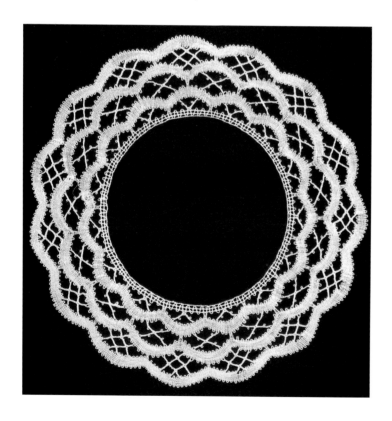

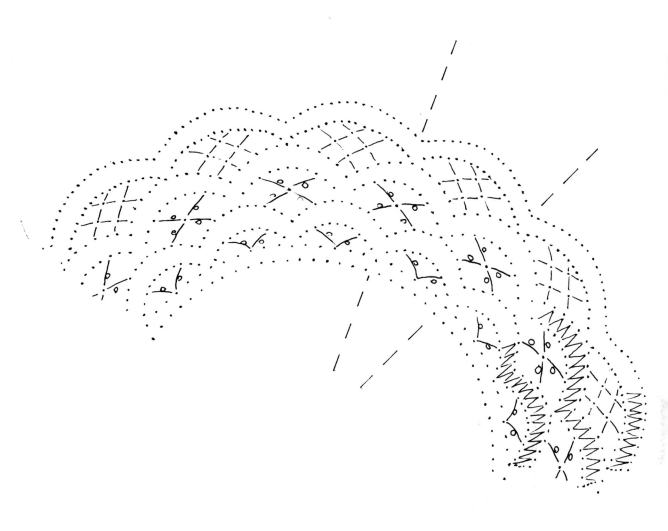

GIRLANDEN *

Diese runde Spitze im Bedford Stil wird entgegen dem Uhrzeigersinn geklöppelt. Im AußenBand werden die Paare für die Füllung, wo es notwendig ist, mitgeführt, während die Paare für die inneren Bänder durch das äußere Band geführt werden, wie in der Darstellung gezeigt. 15 Musterrapporte ergeben einen geschlossenen Ring.

SLINGERS *

Een rond ontwerp in Bedsfordshire stijl, tegen de klok in gewerkt. Het buitenbandje neemt de vullingparen waar nodig mee, terwijl de paren voor de binnenbandjes volgens de werktekening oversteken naar het buitenbandje. Er zijn 15 rapporten nodig voor de hele cirkel.

FESTONS *

Dessin circulaire de style Beds que l'on travaille dans le sens inverse des aiguilles d'une montre. Les paires du fond sont amenées à leur place par le lacet extérieur et les paires pour les lacets intérieurs viennent du lacet extérieur par croisement comme sur le diagramme. 15 répétitions du motif forment un rond complet.

SUMMER DAISIES *

The second in this group of circular edgings is a pretty Beds lace design, with eight-petalled flowers. Eighteen repeats of the pattern are required to complete the circle.

BOBBINS: 24 pairs
THREAD: BOCKENS linen 50

GÄNSEBLÜMCHEN *

Die zweite in dieser Gruppe der runden Einfassungen ist ein hübsches Bedford- Spitzen-Muster mit 8-blättrigen Formschlag-Blüten. Um den Kreis zu schließen, sind 18 Wiederholungen erforderlich.

ZOMERMARGRIETEN *

De tweede in deze groep van ronde randen is een mooi Bedfordshire ontwerp, met 8-bladige bloemen. De cirkel bestaat uit 18 rapporten.

MARGUERITES *

Le second de ce chapitre sur les bordures circulaires est un joli modèle en Beds avec des fleurs à 8 pétales. 18 répétitions du motif forment un rond complet.

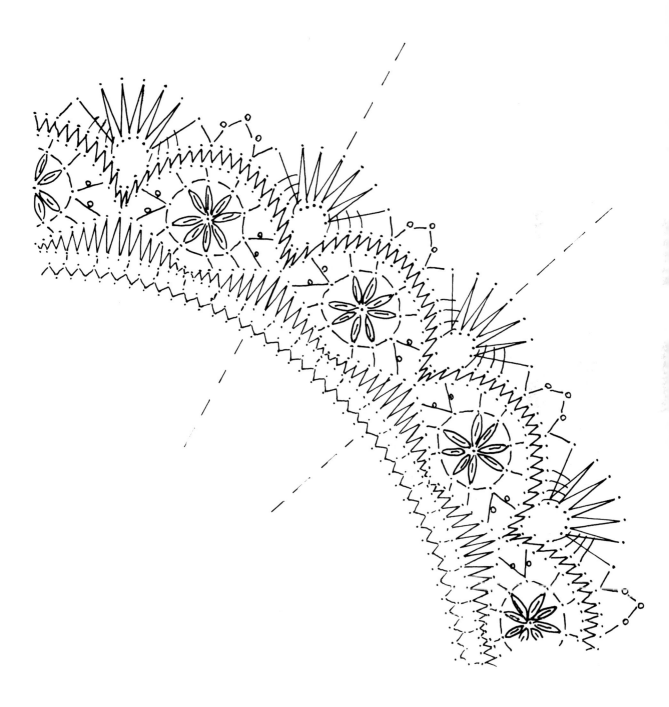

CIRCLES **

This is another circular design, but in Schneeberg techniques. Twelve repeats of the pattern complete the ring. Follow the diagram to work the outer loops, as the plait and picot edge between the repeats is made with 4 pairs, not the usual 2.

BOBBINS: 12 pairs for the
          main shape
          4 pairs for the inner
          braid
THREAD: BOUC Fil de Lin 100

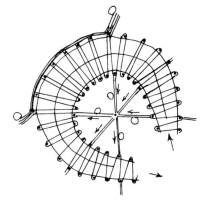

Direction of work for the filling of Circles

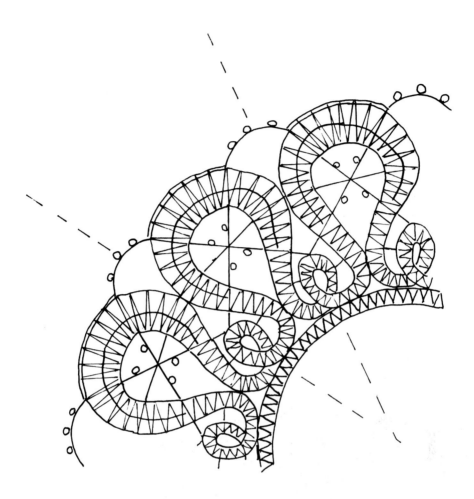

KREISE **

Ein weiterer runder Entwurf -
aber in Schneeberger Technik.
12 Wiederholungen des
Musterrapports schließen den
Ring. Arbeiten Sie den äußeren
Ring nach der Zeichnung, da die
Flechte und der Pikotrand
zwischen den Wiederholungen
mit 4 Paaren, statt der üblichen 2,
geklöppelt wird.

CIRKELS **

Nog een cirkelvormig ontwerp,
maar in Schneebergtechniek. Er
zijn 12 rapporten nodig voor de
hele ring. Volg de werktekening
om de buitenlussen te klossen
want de rand van spijlen en
picots tussen de rapporten is
gemaakt met 4 paar, niet met de
gebruikelijke 2.

RONDS **

Encore un modèle circulaire, cette
fois en Schneeberg. 12 répétitions
du motif forment un rond
complet. Bien suivre le
diagramme pour faire les boucles
extérieures parce que les cordes
de 4 et picots se font avec 4 paires
et non 2 comme d'habitude.

CHAPTER FIVE
LACE FOR WEDDINGS

HOEHZEITSSPITZEN ✳ KANT VOOR
HUWELIJKEN ✳ DENTELLES POUR UN MARIAGE

BOOKMARK *

Take the top support pins out and ease the thread down to obtain a straight edge at the top.

BOBBINS: 18 pairs
THREAD: DMC Special
                Dentelle 80

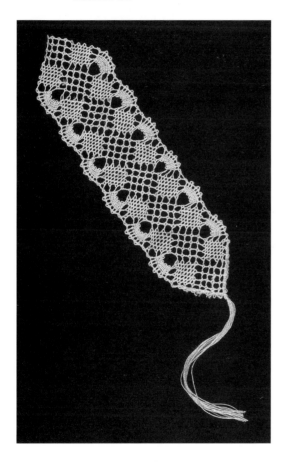

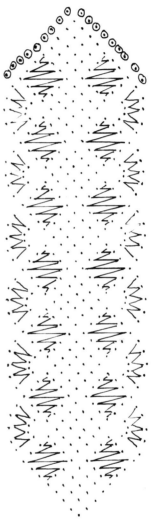

LESEZEICHEN *

Nehmen Sie die Anfangsstecknadeln heraus und schieben den Faden vorsichtig, um eine gerade obere Kante zu erhalten.

BOEKENLEGGER *

Neem de bovenste steunspelden uit de kant en trek de draden voorzichtig naar beneden om een rechte bovenkant te krijgen.

MARQUE-PAGE *

Retirer les épingles du sommet et tirer les paires en place pour avoir un bord droit en haut.

GARTER *

The simple Cluny/torchon design of this garter is echoed in the handkerchief on page 68 and the bookmark on page 65, so the three make a set of pretty gifts. One metre (40 in) of lace is usually enough for the garter.

BOBBINS: 30 pairs
THREAD: DMC Special
Dentelle 80

Narrow ribbon and
elastic to thread
through the centre

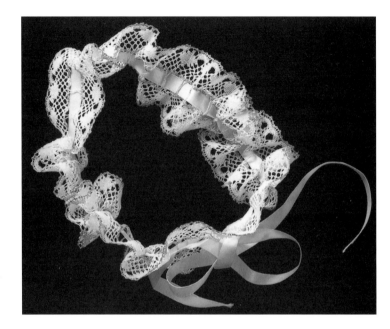

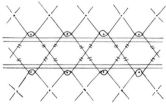

Centre of the Garter

STRUMPFBAND *

Das einfache Cluny/Torchonmuster dieses Strumpfbandes wird beim Taschentuch und dem Lesezeichen, die folgen, wiederholt. Auf diese Weise erhält man ein hübsches Geschenk-Set. Ein Meter Spitze ist im allgemeinen genug für das Strumpfband.

KOUSENBAND *

Het eenvoudige Cluny/Torchon ontwerp van deze kousenband keert terug in de zakdoek en de boekenlegger die nog volgen. Samen vormen deze drie dus een setje leuke geschenkjes. Een meter kant is meestal genoeg voor de kousenband.

LA JARRETIÈRE *

Ce modèle de type Cluny/Torchon fait partie d'une série avec le mouchoir et le marque-page qui suivent, tous les trois feront un joli cadeau. En général 1 mètre de dentelle pour la jarretière suffit.

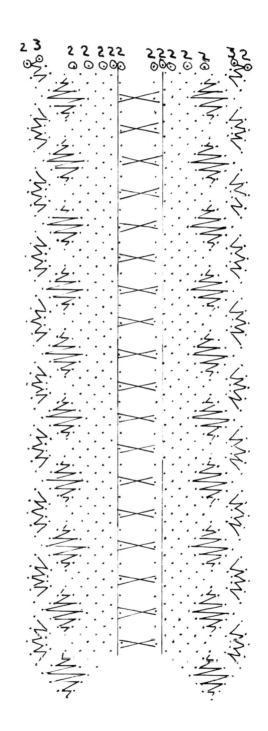

HANDKERCHIEF *

The third design in the set. The pattern matches the garter. If you are going to trim a purchased handkerchief, make the lace at least 1.3 cm (½ in) longer on each side and ease it on.

BOBBINS: 11 pairs
THREAD: DMC Special
          Dentelle 80

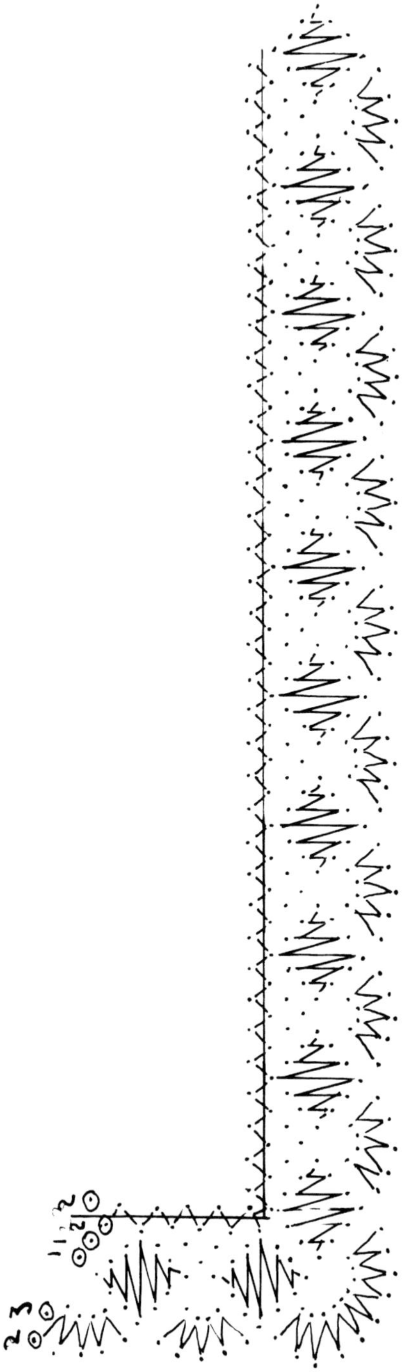

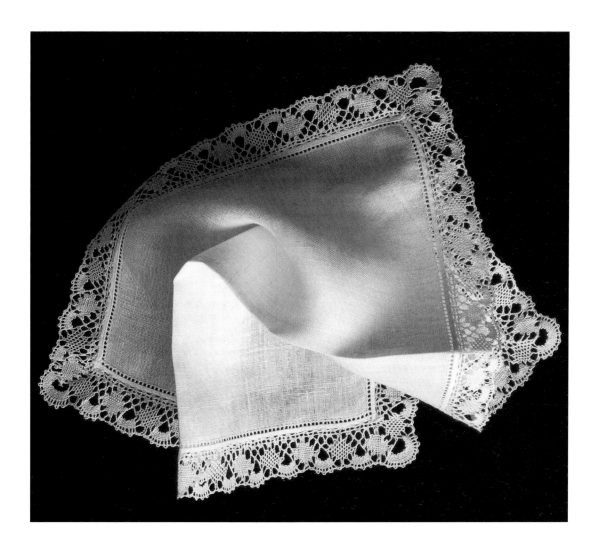

TASCHENTUCH *

Das dritte Stück aus dem Set. Das
Muster paßt zum Strumpfband.
Wenn Sie ein gekauftes
Taschentuch verzieren wollen,
arbeiten Sie die Spitze mindestens
1.3 cm länger an jeder Seite und
nähen Sie sie locker an.

ZAKDOEK *

Het derde ontwerp in de set. Het
patroon past bij de kousenband.
Als u een gekocht zakdoekje gaat
gebruiken, klos dan voor iedere
zijde minstens 1.3 cm meer kant
en zet het losjes aan.

MOUCHOIR *

Troisième de la série. Ce modèle
va avec la jarretière. Si c'est pour
border un mouchoir du
commerce, ajouter environ 1.3 cm
sur chaque côté et la dentelle sera
réajustée au montage.

CROSS *

A simple but elegant design to decorate a veil or the train of a wedding dress. Consider enlarging it, reducing it, or even working it in gold or silver threads.

BOBBINS: 8 pairs
THREAD: BOUC Fil de Lin
    120

KREUZ *

Ein einfaches, aber elegantes Muster, um einen Schleier oder die Schleppe eines Brautkleides zu dekorieren. Man kann es vergrößern, verkleinern oder einfach mit Gold- oder Silbergarn klöppeln.

KRUIS *

Een eenvoudig maar elegant ontwerp om een sluier of de sleep van een bruidsjapon te versieren. Probeer het eens vergroot of verkleind of zelfs in goud- of zilverdraad.

CROIX *

Voici un motif simple et élégant pour décorer un voile ou la traîne de la robe de mariée. Essayer de l'agrandir, la réduire ou même de la faire en or ou argent.

HEAD-DRESSES *

Here is a set of velvet and pearl head-dresses for the bride or bridesmaids. All the designs are either sewn on to plain commercial hairbands, or stuck on using fabric glue.

KOPFSCHMUCK *

Es folgen verschiedene Haarreifen aus Samt und Perlen für die Braut oder die Brautjungfern. Alle Muster sind entweder auf einen gekauften, flachen Haarreifen aufgenäht oder mit Textilkleber aufgeklebt.

HAARBANDEN *

Dit is een set fluwelen haarbanden met pareltjes voor bruid of bruidsmeisjes. Alle ontwerpen zijn ofwel op gekochte haarbanden genaaid of, met textiellijm, er op geplakt.

COIFFES *

Voici une série de coiffes en velours et perles pour la mariée et les demoiselles d'honneur. Tous ces motifs peuvent être directement cousus sur des serre-tête du commerce, ou collés avec de la colle à tissu.

NARROW HEAD-DRESS *

The centre bead is added as shown on the diagram for the large Christmas tree (see page 28), at every other pinhole, instead of using a pin. Velvet ribbon is woven through the centre, so that the beads are uppermost and the alternate crossed threads are underneath.

BOBBINS: 6 pairs
THREAD: DMC Cordonnet 60
3.5 mm beads
10 cm (⅜ in)
wide velvet ribbon

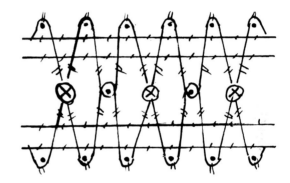

Working diagram for the Head-dress

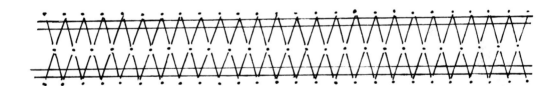

SCHMALER HAARREIF *

Die Mittelperlen werden eingeklöppelt, wie es in der Abbildung zum großen Weihnachtsbaum (siehe S. 28) gezeigt wird, an jedem zweiten Nadelpunkt anstelle einer Nadel. Durch die Mitte wird ein Samtband gewebt, so daß die mit Perlen besetzten Kreuzungen obenauf liegen und die übrigen unterhalb.

SMALLE HAARBAND *

De kralen in het midden worden, als in de werktekening voor de Grote kerstboom (zie pagina 28), om het andere speldengat mee gewerkt, in plaats van de speld. Een fluwelen band wordt door het midden geweven, zo dat de parels aan de bovenzijde liggen en de tussenliggende gekruiste draden onder.

PETITE COIFFE *

La perle au centre se met comme sur le diagramme du grand sapin de Noël (voir page 28), et à tous les autres trous d'épingle pour remplacer l'épingle. Un fil velours est tissé au centre pour surélever les perles et les croisements de fils sont dessous.

BEADED EDGE HEAD-DRESS *

For the centre beads, follow instructions for the narrow head-dress. The edge beads are strung on to a single thread, which is worked as a gimp. One bead slides up between the workers on each outward journey only.

BOBBINS: 8 pairs and 2
single for the beads
THREAD: DMC Cordonnet 60
3 mm beads for the
centre
3.5 mm beads for
the edge

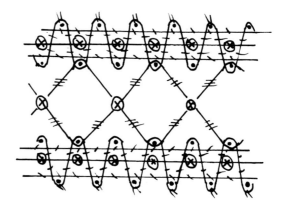

Working diagram for the Head-dress

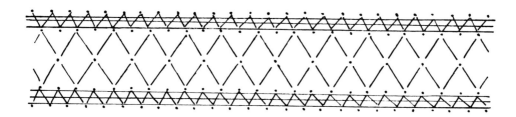

PERLENBESETZTER HAARREIF *

Bei den Perlen in der Mitte arbeiten Sie gemäß der Anleitung des schmalen Haarreifs.
Die Randperlen werden auf einen einzelnen Faden aufgezogen, der als Konturfaden geklöppelt wird. Bei jedem Weg nach außen läßt man eine Perle zwischen das Laufpaar rutschen.

HAARBAND MET PARELRAND *

Volg voor de middenkralen de instructie voor de smalle haarband. De randkralen worden op een enkele draad geregen, die als sierdraad wordt gewerkt. Bij iedere toer naar buiten wordt slechts ÇÇn kraal tussen de lopers gelegd.

BORD PERLÉ DE COIFFE *

Suivre les instructions de la petite coiffe pour les perles du milieu. Les perles du bord, les enfiler sur un fil qui sera travaillé comme un cordon. Une seule perle passe entre les voyageurs seulement sur le trajet vers l'extérieur.

DIAMOND BEADED HEAD-DRESS *

The diagram shows the positioning of the beaded gimp that forms the diamond shape.

BOBBINS: 12 pairs
THREAD: DMC Cordonnet 60
2 single beaded
threads for diamond
shapes

3 mm beads

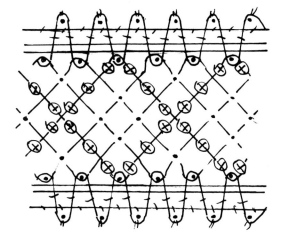

Working diagram for the Head-dress

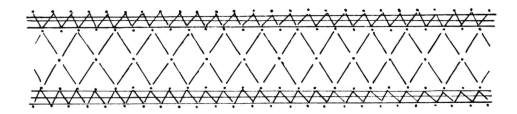

HAARREIF MIT RAUTENMUSTER *

Die Abbildung zeigt die Positionierung des mit Perlen versehenen Konturfadens, der das Rautenmuster bildet.

HAARBAND MET PARELS IN RUITEN *

De werktekening laat de plaats zien van de sierdraad met kralen, die de ruiten vormt.

LOSANGE PERLÉ DE LA COIFFE *

Suivre le diagramme pour voir le passage du cordon perlé qui souligne un losange.

PARASOL, FAN AND HORSESHOE SET **

This three-piece set is constructed with simple braid designs that have been decorated with fine torchon frills. The details for each braid are shown in the diagrams. Note that the chain-stitch and stem-stitch thick threads are depicted singly; for all other threads, one line represents one pair.

Simple torchon fillings have been used, but these can be altered as required. The lace could be lined with the fabric from the bridesmaids' dresses. Narrow embroidery ribbon is threaded through the frills to draw up the gathers.

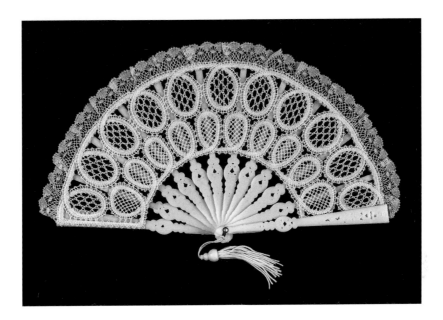

SONNENSCHIRM, FÄCHER UND HUFEISEN **

Dieses 3-er-Set ist aus einfachen Bändermustern aufgebaut, die mit zarten Torchonspitzen verziert worden sind. Die Einzelheiten für jedes Band werden in den Fadenverlaufsskizzen gezeigt. Beachten Sie, daß die dicken Kett- und Stielstichfäden einzeln abgebildet sind; für alle anderen Fäden gilt: eine Linie gleich ein Paar.

Es wurden einfache Torchonfüllungen verwendet, die aber nach Belieben geändert werden können. Die Spitze kann mit dem Stoff von den Kleidern der Brautjungfern unterfüttert werden. Ein schmales Schmuckband wird durch die Torchonspitze gezogen, um sie in Falten zu legen.

PARASOL, WAAIER EN HOEFIJZER, SET **

Deze driedelige set is opgebouwd uit eenvoudige bandjes, die zijn versierd met volants van fijne Torchon. De details van ieder bandje zijn gegeven in de werktekeningen. Let op: de dikke draden van kettingsteek en steelsteek zijn apart getekend; voor alle andere draden geldt: ÇÇn lijn stelt een paar voor.
Er zijn eenvoudige torchongronden gebruikt als vulling, maar die kunnen naar believen worden vervangen door andere. De kant zou gevoerd kunnen worden met de stof van de jurken van de bruidsmeisjes. Smal handwerklint is door de volants geregen om deze te rimpelen.

OMBRELLE, ÉVENTAIL ET FER À CHEVAL **

Cette série de trois pièces n'est autre qu'un travail de lacets sertis de fins volants en Torchon. Les détails de chaque lacet sont sur le diagramme. Attention, les traits du point chaînette et du point tige représente 1 fil, sinon 1 trait représente 1 paire.
Des fonds simples en Torchon ont été choisis mais on peut les modifier à sa guise. On peut doubler la dentelle avec le tissu des robes des demoiselles d'honneur. On peut broder aux rubans très fins sur les fronces des volants.

PARASOL **

Buy a parasol from a specialist bridal shop and remove the machine-made lace.

**Parasol 16 cm (6 in)
radius**

Centre ring
BOBBINS: 5 pairs
THREAD: DMC Cordonnet 60

Middle braid
BOBBINS: 6 pairs
THREAD: DMC Cordonnet 60

Outer braid
BOBBINS: 8 pairs
THREAD: DMC Cordonnet 60

Gimp
BOBBINS: 2 pairs
THREAD: DMC Coton Perlé 5

Gimp
BOBBINS: 2 pairs
THREAD: DMC Coton Perlé 5

Frill
(length 1½ times the parasol's
circumference)
BOBBINS: 28 pairs
THREAD: DMC Broder
          Machine 50

Position of threads for the Parasol

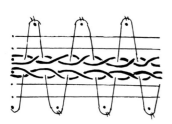

Centre braid for parasol

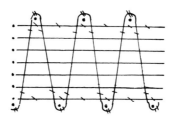

Middle braid for parasol

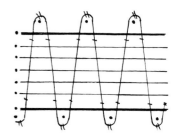

Outer braid for parasol

SONNENSCHIRM **

Kaufen Sie einen Schirm mit
16 cm Durchmesser in einem
Brautmodengeschäft und
entfernen Sie die
Maschinenspitze. Folgende
Materialien werden benötigt:

PARASOL **

Koop in een speciaalzaak voor
bruidskleding een parasol van
16 cm en verwijder de machinale
kant. De volgende materialen zijn
nodig:

OMBRELLE **

Acheter une ombrelle de 16 cm
de diamètre chez un spécialiste de
robes de mariées et retirer la
dentelle mécanique. Voir la liste
des fournitures ci-dessous:

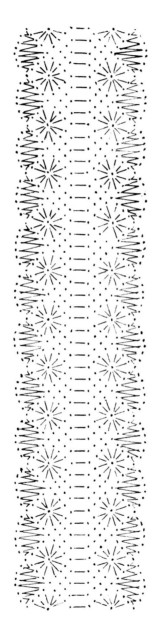

Parasol frill

Fan frill

FAN **

Buy a commercially produced fan from a specialist bridal shop and remove the machine-made lace, leaving the sticks.

Fan 15 cm (6 in) radius

Braid
BOBBINS: 6 pairs
THREAD: DMC Cordonnet 60
and
BOBBINS: 1 pair
THREAD: DMC Coton Perlé 5

Frill
(1½ times the length of the top, rounded edge)
BOBBINS: 14 pairs
THREAD: DMC Broder
             Machine 50

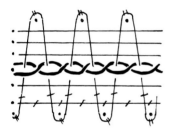

Braid for fan

FÄCHER **

Von einem fertigen, in einem Brautmodengeschäft gekauften Fächer entfernen Sie die Maschinenspitze und verwenden nur das Fächergestell.

WAAIER **

Koop in een speciaalzaak voor bruidskleding een waaier en verwijder de machinale kant, waarna u de benen overhoudt.

EVENTAIL **

Acheter un éventail dans une boutique pour mariées et retirer la dentelle mécanique pour ne garder que la monture.

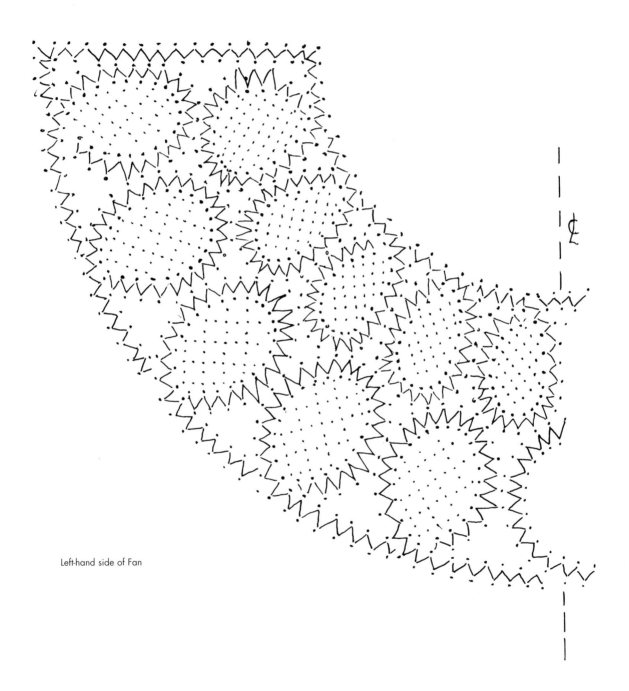

Left-hand side of Fan

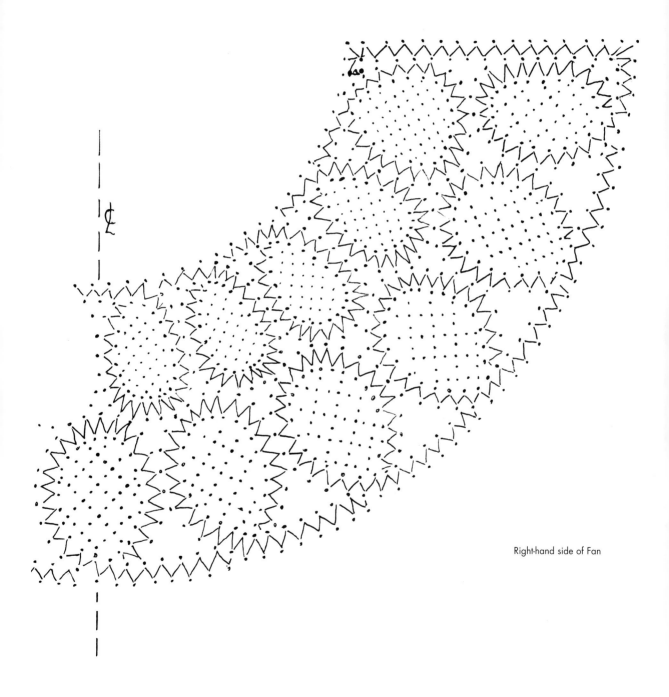

Right-hand side of Fan

HORSESHOE **

Make the horseshoe base by tracing the shape of the pricking on to stiff card. Then covered this with ribbon or material. The frill must be twice the length of the outside edge. The braid changes to half-stitch when the loops are reached, with one of the gimp threads being used as the outside of the loops.

Braid
BOBBINS: 5 pairs
THREAD: DMC Cordonnet 60

Gimp
BOBBINS: 1 pair
THREAD: DMC Coton Perlé 5

Frill
BOBBINS: 11 pairs
THREAD: DMC Broder
Machine 50

Handle
2 ribbon roses and a length of ribbon

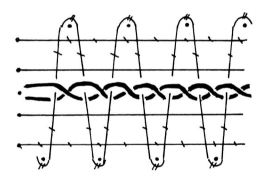

Position of threads for the Horseshoe

HUFEISEN **

Übertragen Sie zunächst die Umrisse des Klöppelbriefes auf festen Karton, um den „Kern" des Hufeisens zu bekommen. Dieser wird dann mit Band oder Stoff bezogen. Die Torchonrüsche muß die zweifache Länge des Außenrandes haben.

HOEFIJZER **

Maak het hoefijzer door de omtrek van de prikking over te nemen op stevig karton. Dit wordt dan overtrokken met lint of stof. De volant moet twee maal zo lang zijn als de buitenkant van het hoefijzer. Het bandje gaat bij de lussen over in netslag, waarbij ÇÇn van de sierdraden gebruikt wordt als buitenrand van de lussen.

FER À CHEVAL **

Faire un dessin de base sur une carte. Recouvrir avec des rubans ou du tissu. Le volant doit être le double de la longueur du pourtour extérieur. Quand on atteint les boucles, changer en grille, et un des cordons sert pour l'extérieur des boucles.

Horseshoe braid

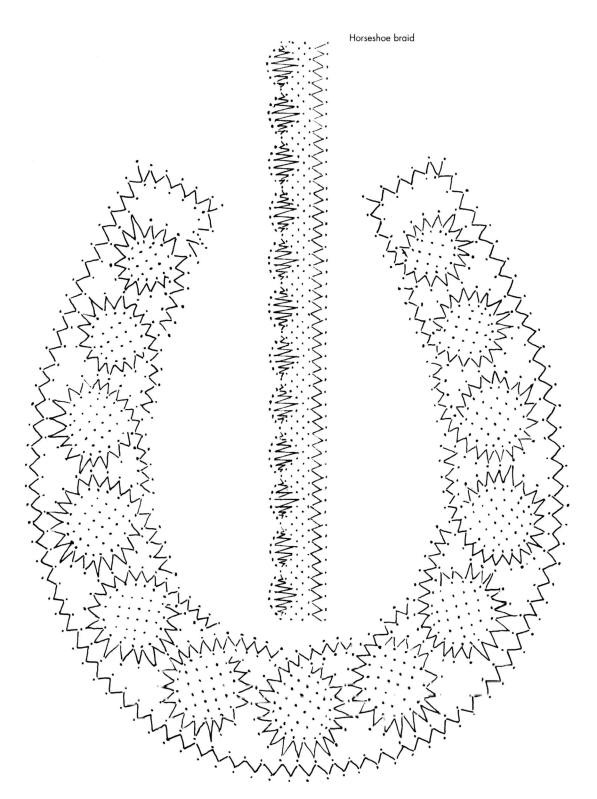

CHAPTER SIX
PICTURE FRAMES

BILDUMRAHMUNGEN ✳ SCHILDERIJLIJSTJES
✳ ENCADREMENT DE DENTELLE

TRAY WITH LACEMAKER *

This narrow torchon design with alternating fan and shell repeats is worked in very dark green to echo one of the colours in the cross-stitch embroidery.

BOBBINS: 9 pairs
THREAD: DMC Broder
Machine 30

TABLETT MIT KLÖPPLERIN *

Das schmale Torchonband mit abwechselndem Fächer und Muschelrapprt ist in sehr dunklem Grün geklöppelt, um eine Farbe aus der Kreuzstichstickerei zu wiederholen.

BLAADJE MET KANTKLOSSTER *

Dit smalle Torchonontwerp met afwisselend een waaier en een schelp is in zeer donker groen geklost, aansluitend bij ÇÇn van de kleuren uit het borduurwerkje.

PLATEAU DE LA DENTELLIÈRE *

Ce motif étroit en Torchon où s'alternent éventails et coquilles est fait en vert foncé pour relever une des couleurs de la broderie au point de croix.

'ROSE' TAPESTRY FRAME *

Note that the 'head' is facing inwards for decoration. The design is large-scale, and the thick thread gives it a texture similar to that of the wool tapestry it frames.

BOBBINS: 10 pairs
THREAD: BOUC Fil de lin 50

WANDBEHANG „ROSE" *

Beachten Sie, daß der „Kopf" der Spitze hier zu Dekorationszwecken nach innen angeordnet ist. Die Spitze ist grob strukturiert und paßt sich durch das verwendete dicke Garn in der Struktur dem Wollgobelin an.

LIJSTJE VOOR GEBORDUURDE ROOS *

Merk op dat de "buitenrand" als versiering aan de binnenkant ligt. Het ontwerp is wat grover en door het dikke garen lijkt de structuur op die van de borduurwol.

"ROSE", CADRE POUR TAPISSERIE *

Bien placer la "tête" de la dentelle vers l'intérieur pour la décoration. Le dessin est agrandi, et les gros fils donnent une texture semblable à celle de la tapisserie en laine du centre.

FRILL FOR SMALL ROUND FRAME DESIGN *

This is another simple torchon design with a French fan 'head'. The rose ground area reflects the texture of the AIDA embroidery material. A single gimp thread is woven through the foot to gather the frill. Work a length double the circumference.

BOBBINS: 6 pairs
THREAD: DMC Broder
Machine 30
1 single DMC Coton
Perlé 5 for the gimp

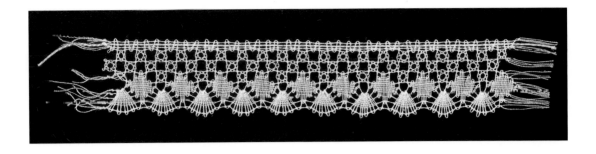

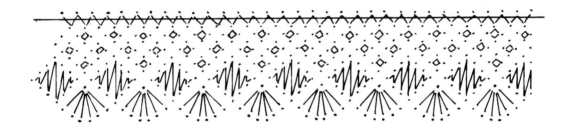

SPITZENRÜSCHE FÜR SCHMALEN RUNDEN RAHMEN *

Dies ist ein anderes, einfaches Torchonmuster mit einem französischen Fächer-"Kopf". Der Rohrstuhlgrund gibt die Struktur des AIDA-Stickstoffes wieder. Ein einzelner Konturfaden wird durch den geraden Rand gewebt, um die Spitze zu rüschen. Arbeiten Sie die zweifache Länge des Umfanges.

VOLANT VOOR EEN KLEINE RONDE LIJST *

Ook dit is een eenvoudige Torchon met als buitenrand een Paddepoot. Het deel met de Viergegrond reflecteert de structuur van de Aãdastof, waarop geborduurd is. Een enkele sierdraad is door de zelfkant geregen om de volant te rimpelen. Klos een lengte van twee keer de omtrek.

VOLANT POUR ENTOURER UN PETIT ROND *

Voici un autre modèle simple avec un éventail en "tête". Le fond mariage équilibre la texture du tissu à broder Aïda. Un cordon unique passe dans le pied pour froncer le volant. Doubler la longueur de la circonférence à garnir.

'KITTEN' FRAME *

This continuous looped edge frame is an extension of the parasol/fan/horseshoe set (see pages 76–85) if used for a wedding photograph.

BOBBINS: 5 pairs
THREAD: BOUC fil de Lin 100
1 pair DMC Coton
Perlé 5 for the gimp

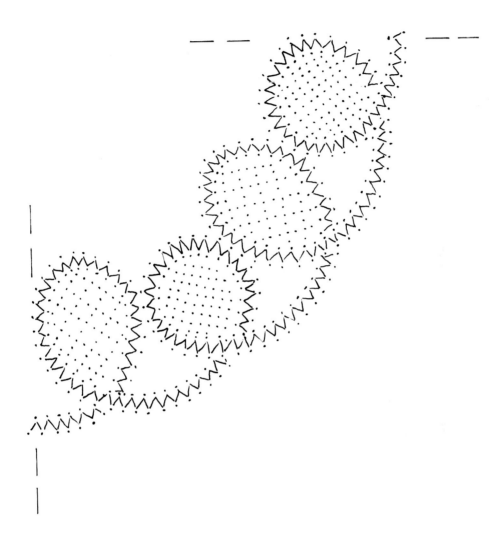

„KÄTZCHEN"-RAHMEN *

Dieser Rahmen mit einem
fortlaufend verschlungenen Band
wird mit einem Hochzeitsfoto
zur Erweiterung des
Sonnenschirm-Fächer-Hufeisen-
Sets (vgl. S. 76–85).

POEZENLIJST *

Deze lijst met een rand van
doorlopende lussen is, indien
gebruikt voor een trouwfoto, een
aanvulling van de
parasol/waaier/hoefijzer set.

CADRE "CHATON" *

Cette bordure dentelée au mètre
est une suite de la série
ombrelle/éventail/fer à cheval
(voir pages 76–85) pour
l'utilisation d'une photo de
mariage.

GRANNY'S PHOTO FRAME *

This makes a delicate frame for that special photograph. The outer edge is straight
and the Cluny-type inner edge is decorated with picots.

BOBBINS: 12 pairs
THREAD: BOUC fil de lin 100

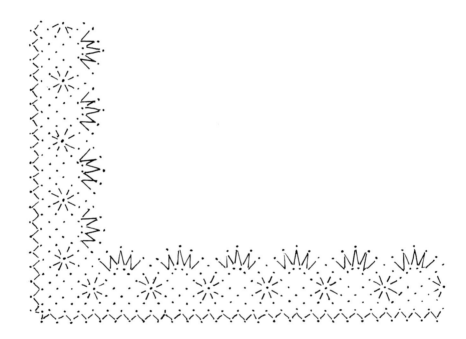

GROSSMUTTERS BILDERRAHMEN *

Diese Spitze bildet einen zarten
Rahmen für solch ein besonderes
Foto. Der äußere Rand ist gerade
und der Cluny-ähnliche innere
Rand ist mit Pikots verziert.

GROOTMOEDERS FOTOLIJSTJE *

Dit is een fijn lijstje voor die
speciale foto. De buitenrand is
recht en de binnenrand in Cluny-
stijl is versierd met picots.

CADRE POUR LA PHOTO DE MAMY *

Voilà un joli cadre pour une
tendre photo. Le bord extérieur
est droit et le bord intérieur de
style Cluny est décoré de picots.

IRISES BORDER **

Here is a frame with a difference. The base is an attractive torchon design, while the sides and top are a simple narrow edge of Dieppe ground (with the straight edge towards the centre). Work the narrow sides first and add the extra pairs of bobbins as you reach the base. For the iris pricking, see page 24.

BOBBINS: 8 pairs for the sides, increasing to 18 pairs for the base

THREAD: DMC Broder Machine 30

SCHWERTLILIEN UMRAHMUNG **

Hier haben wir einen Rahmen mit einer Abweichung. Den unteren Rand bildet ein reizendes Torchonmuster, während die Seiten und der obere Rand eine einfache Randspitze im Dieppe-Grund (mit geradem inneren Rand) sind. Die schmalen Seiten werden zuerst geklöppelt und zusätzliche Paare in die Arbeit hereingenommen, wenn Sie am unteren Rand ankommen. Den zugehörigen Klöppelbrief für die Schwertlilien finden Sie auf S. 24.

RAND VOOR IRISSEN **

Dit lijstje is een beetje bijzonder. De onderkant is een fraaie Torchontekening, terwijl de zijkanten en de bovenkant bestaan uit een eenvoudige smalle rand van Dieppegrond (met de rechte rand aan de binnenkant). Klos de smalle zijden eerst en voeg de extra paren toe als u bij de onderkant bent. Voor de prikking van de Irissen: zie pagina 24.

BORDURE AUX IRIS **

Voilà un encadrement différent. En bas, un joli motif Torchon, sur les côtés et le haut un petit entre-deux en point Dieppe (avec le bord droit vers le centre). Commencer par les côtés puis ajouter des paires pour la base. Pour le modèle des iris, voir page 24.

FLOWER GARDEN **

A mixture of Bruges flowers and Schneeberg leaves gives this oval frame a fresh
look. It can be worked in realistic colours to complement the cross-stitch lacemaker
design. The leaves here do not need the extra strength of a traditional plaited edge.

Flowers
BOBBINS: 10 pairs
THREAD: DMC Special
               Dentelle 80

Leaves and frame
BOBBINS: 5 pairs
BOBBINS: DMC Special
               Dentelle 80

BLUMENGARTEN **

Eine Mischung aus Brügger
Blumen und Schneeberger
Blättern gibt diesem ovalen
Rahmen ein frisches Aussehen.
Er kann in nüchternen Farben
gearbeitet werden, um das
Kreuzstichmotiv der Klöpplerin zu
unterstreichen. Die Blätter
brauchen hier in diesem Fall keine
die zusätzliche Verstärkung durch
einen traditionellen Flechtenrand.

BLOEMENTUIN **

Een mengeling van Brugse
bloemen en Schneeberg bladeren
geeft deze ovale lijst een
verfrissend uiterlijk. Hij kan in
realistische kleuren worden
gewerkt om bij de geborduurde
kantklosster te passen. De
bladeren hebben hier niet de
extra stevigheid nodig van een
traditionele gevlochten rand.

JARDIN FLEURI **

Un décor de feuilles ravissant
pour cet ovale en Fleuri de
Bruges et Schneeberg. On peut
mettre des couleurs naturelles
pour aller avec la broderie au
point de croix. Par contre ici, on
n'a pas besoin du renfort en
corde des bords.

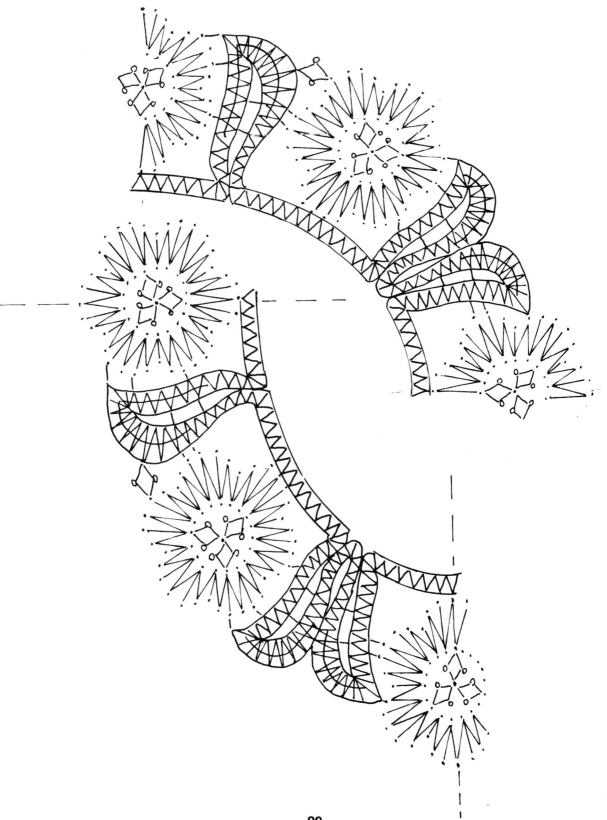

CHAPTER SEVEN
EARRINGS

OHRRINGE ✱ OORBELLEN
✱ BOUCLES D'OREILLES

LITTLE STARS *

Start at the top with 2 pairs, which are plaited to the centre adding 1 pair for the outer ring and one for the inner ring. Where the plaits and single pairs cross, work 3-pair crossings. It is advisable with all the earrings in this chapter to finish the earrings, before taking them off the pillow, by spraying them with unperfumed hair lacquer, starch or other stiffener to maintain their shape.

BOBBINS: 4 pairs
THREAD: DMC Broder
Machine 50
2 small pearl beads
(sewn on after
completion)

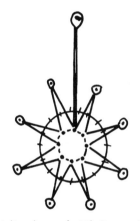

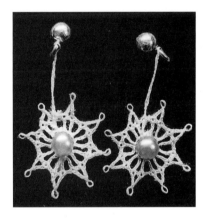

Working diagram for Little Stars earrings

KLEINE STERNE *

Beginnen Sie oben mit zwei Paaren und klöppeln damit eine Flechte bis zur Sternenmitte. Fügen Sie ein Paar für den äußeren und eines für den inneren Ring hinzu. Wo die Flechten und Einzelpaare sich kreuzen, wird eine 3-paarige Verbindung geklöppelt. Es ist ratsam die Ohrringe zu appretieren, bevor man sie vom Kissen abnimmt, indem sie mit unparfümiertem Haarlack, Stärke oder sonstiger Appretur eingesprüht werden, damit sie ihre Form behalten.

STERRETJES *

Begin bovenaan met twee paar, die naar het midden worden gevlochten, waarbij ÇÇn paar wordt bijgelegd voor de buitenring en ÇÇn paar voor de binnenring. Werk waar vlecht en enkele paren elkaar kruisen, kruisingen voor drie paren. Het is wenselijk de oorringen, alvorens ze van het kussen te halen, te behandelen met ongeparfumeerde haarlak, stijfsel of andere versteviger, zodat ze hun vorm behouden.

PETITES ETOILES *

Commencer en haut avec 2 paires qui vont au centre en corde de 4, on ajoute alors 1 paire pour le cercle extérieur et 1 paire pour le cercle intérieur. Au croisement des cordes et des paires isolées, suivre la technique croisement de 6. Le travail terminé, ne pas oublier d'empeser la dentelle encore sous épingles avec une laque à cheveux sans parfum en amidon ou autre pour bien garder la forme.

HEARTS *

A simple tape lace shape.

BOBBINS: 6 pairs
THREAD: DMC Broder
Machine 50

Braid used for Hearts earrings

HERZEN *

Ein einfaches
Bänderspitzenmuster.

HARTEN *

Een eenvoudige vorm van
bandkant.

COEURS *

Un modèle en lacet.

FISHES *

Begin at the tail and work in continuous braid to the other tip, ending with secured hidden threads as worked in Schneeberg lace. The filling is plaited.

BOBBINS: 5 pairs of bobbins
              4 pairs for the filling
              1 single gimp
THREAD: DMC Broder
              Machine 50
              DMC Coton Perlé
              12 for the gimp

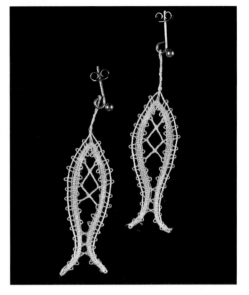

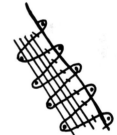

Position of threads for Fishes earrings

FISCHE *

Man fängt an der einen Schwanzflosse an und arbeitet ein fortlaufendes Band bis zur anderen Flossenspitze, das im Leinenschlag endet, hinter dem die gebündelten und verknoteten Fäden wie bei der Schneeberger Spitze versteckt werden. Die Füllung besteht aus Flechten.

VISJES *

Begin bij de staart en werk als doorlopend bandje naar de andere punt, eindigend met verborgen vastgezette draden, als in Schneebergkant. De vulling is gevlochten.

POISSONS *

Commencer par la queue et travailler en lacet jusqu'à l'autre bout en finissant en fils cachés façon Schneeberg. Faire un fond en corde de 4.

CROSSES **

These are a little fiddly. The outer points are worked using Bruges pivot pins and the inner corners with the Schneeberg turning stitch.

BOBBINS: 5 pairs
THREAD: DMC Broder
Machine 50

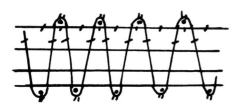

Crosses braid

KREUZE **

Diese sind ein bißchen knifflig. An den äußeren Punkten werden Brügger Pikot- Nadeln verwendet und die inneren Ecken mit Schneeberger Umkehrschlag geklöppelt.

KRUISJES **

Deze zijn een beetje lastig. De punten aan de buitenkant zijn op de Brugse manier gemaakt met de krulbewerking, en de binnenhoeken met de omkeerslag volgens de Schneebergtechniek.

CROIX **

C'est un peu minutieux. Aux points extérieurs utiliser le point pivot de la technique Fleuri de Bruges et dans les coins intérieurs faire le point tournant Schneeberg.

SCROLLS **

These are slightly complicated. Beads are threaded on a gimp for the centre.

BOBBINS: 6 pairs for the braid
1 single gimp

THREAD: DMC Broder
Machine 50
DMC Coton Perlé
12 for the gimp

12 seed beads

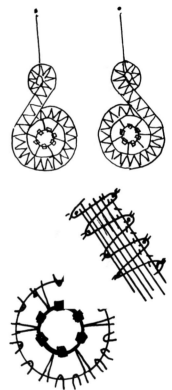

Braid and bead positions for Scrolls

SCHNÖRKEL **

Diese sind etwas kompliziert. Für
die Mitte werden Perlen
aufgefädelt.

KRULLEN **

Deze zijn een beetje ingewikkeld.
De kralen voor het midden zijn
op een sierdraad geregen.

VOLUTES **

C'est assez compliqué. On enfile
des perles sur un cordon pour le
centre.

DOLPHINS **

Start each dolphin at the nose, using 4 pairs and working ten-stick (rib) with no pins. The gimps and an extra 4 pairs are then added as in Honiton lace, except that the gimps form the outermost thread and are used alone rather than with a thin thread to make a pair. The main body is formed by working 4 pairs whole stitch and 3 pairs half-stitch to give a lighter effect on the back. The half-stitch area is marked with dotted lines on the diagram. The tail ends are tied and cut to form tiny tufts.

BOBBINS: 8 pairs
            1 gimp pair

THREAD: DMC Broder
           Machine 50
           DMC Coton Perlé
           12 for the gimps

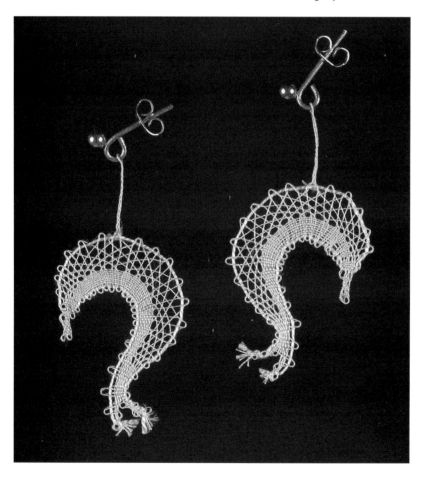

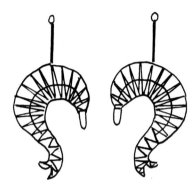

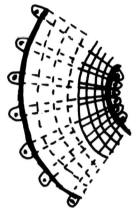

Dolphin thread positions

DELPHINE **

Beginnen Sie jeden Delphin mit 4
Paaren an der Nase und arbeiten
Sie eine Rippe ohne Nadeln. Die
Konturfäden und 4 weitere Paare
werden dann wie bei Honiton-
Spitze hinzugefügt, außer daß die
Konturfäden die äußeren Fäden
bilden und besser einzeln
verwendet werden als mit einem
dünnen Faden ein Paar zu bilden.
Der Hauptkörper wird geformt,
indem man mit 2 Paaren
Leinenschlag und 3 Paaren
Halbschlag, um eine hellere
Wirkung auf dem Rücken zu
haben. Der Halbschlagbereich
wird in der Zeichnung mit
punktierten Linien markiert. Die
Schwanzenden werden zu kleinen
Bündeln verknotet und
abgeschnitten.

DOLFIJNEN **

Begin elke dolfijn bij de neus en
klos met 4 paar een ribje zonder
spelden. Dan worden de
sierdraden en 4 extra paren op de
Honitonmanier ingelegd, met dit
verschil, dat de sierdraden
helemaal aan de buitenkant liggen
en allÇÇn worden geklost in
plaats van samen met een dunne
draad als een paar. Het lijf wordt
gevormd door 4 paar in
linnenslag te klossen en 3 paar in
netslag, voor een lichter effect op
de rug. Het netslagdeel is in de
werktekening aangegeven met
stippellijnen. De staarteindjes
worden geknoopt en afgeknipt
waardoor kleine kwastjes
ontstaan.

DAUPHINS **

Commencer chaque dauphin par
le nez avec 4 paires en lacet
contour sans épingle. Ensuite
ajouter le cordon et 4 paires façon
Honiton sauf pour le cordon qui
travaille seul et non pas en paire
cordon avec un fil fin. Le corps
est fait avec 4 paires en toile et 3
paires en grille pour donner un
effet plus léger sur le dos. La
partie en grille se voit en pointillé
sur le diagramme. Les bouts de
queue sont noués et coupés net
pour donner un effet de petites
touffes.

SWANS **

Begin at the beak with 2 pairs and work a tally adding the extra 4 pairs and 1 gimp pair as in the Dolphin design. The eye is formed by working a Bruges eyelet hole, and decorative twists are made by the worker pair to lighten the underbody. The filling is Dieppe ground, worked without pins.

BOBBINS: 6 pairs
1 gimp pair
THREAD: DMC Broder Machine 50 or other of equivalent thickness
DMC Coton Perlé 12 for the gimp

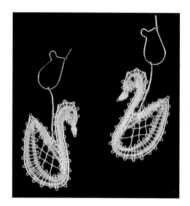

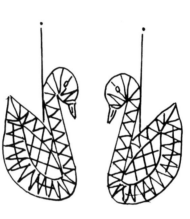

SCHWÄNE **

Man fängt am Schnabel mit 2 Paaren an und arbeitet einen Formschlag. Es werden wie bei den Delphinen 4 weitere Paare, eines davon ist ein Konturpaar, hinzugenommen.
Das Auge entsteht, indem man ein Loch klöppelt (vgl. Brügger Blumenwerk). Um die Bauchseite aufzulockern, werden zusätzliche Dreher mit dem Laufpaar gemacht. Der für die Füllung verwendete Dieppe-Grund wird ohne Nadeln gearbeitet.

ZWANEN **

Begin bij de snavel met 2 paar en klos een vormslag, waarbij de 4 extra paren en het sierdraadpaar worden ingehangen zoals bij de Dolfijnen. Het oog wordt gevormd door een Brugs openluchtje te klossen, en om de onderkant van het lijf wat luchtiger te maken wordt het looppaar gedraaid.
De vulling in Dieppegrond is zonder spelden geklost.

CYGNES **

Commencer sur le bec avec 2 paires et faire un point d'esprit puis ajouter 4 paires et le cordon comme pour le dauphin. Pour l'oeil faire un trou façon ajour en Bruges et pour aérer le ventre faire des torsions des voyageurs. Faire le fond Dieppe sans épingle.

LINKED RINGS ***

Each ring requires 5 pairs and 1 pair of gimps worked in stem stitch for the centre. The three rings are worked simultaneously.

BOBBINS: 15 pairs
3 gimp pairs
THREAD: DMC Broder
Machine 50
DMC Coton Perlé
12 for the gimps

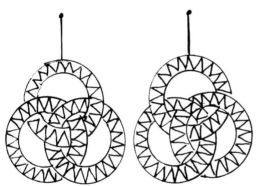

VERBUNDENE RINGE ***

Jeder Ring erfordert 5 Paare und 1 Konturfadenpaar, das als Bandmitte im Stielstich gearbeitet wird. Die drei Ringe werden gleichzeitig geklöppelt.

VERBONDEN RINGEN ***

Voor iedere ring zijn 5 paar nodig, en een in steelsteek geklost sierdraadpaar voor het midden. De drie ringen worden gelijktijdig geklost.

LES ANNEAUX UNIS ***

Chaque anneau se fait avec 5 paires et 1 paire de cordon que l'on travaille en lacet contour pour le centre. Les trois anneaux se font en même temps.

CHAPTER EIGHT
HANDKERCHIEFS

TASCHENTÜCHER ✳ ZAKDOEKJES
✳ MOUCHOIRS

CORNER IN SCHNEEBERG LACE *

A delicate corner; this can be worked as a single piece, or as four separate corners linked, if required, by a wavy edge.

BOBBINS: 6 pairs
THREAD: DMC Special
          Dentelle 80

ECKE IN SCHNEEBERGER SPITZE *

Eine zarte Ecke; diese kann als Einzelstück gearbeitet werden oder viermal, um dann, falls gewünscht, mit einem wellenförmigen Rand miteinander verbunden zu werden.

HOEKJE IN SCHNEEBERG KANT *

Een fijn hoekje, dat als enkel stuk kan worden gemaakt of als vier aparte hoeken, eventueel verbonden door een golvende rand.

COIN EN SCHNEEBERG *

C'est un coin élégant qui peut être unique ou bien faire les quatre coins qui seront réunis si besoin, par une bordure de vagues.

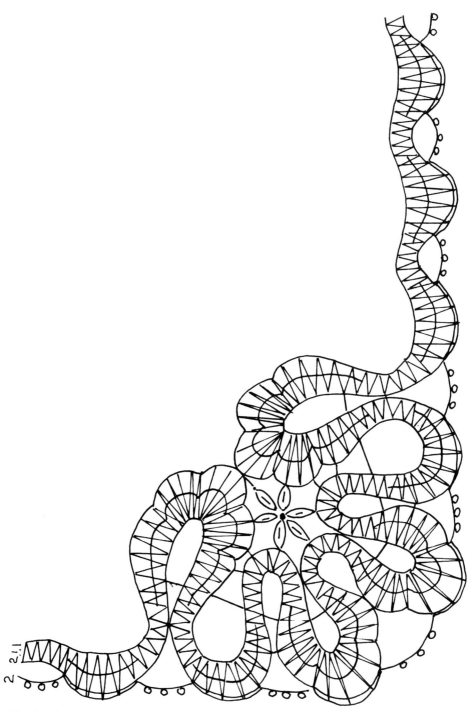

Corner in Schneeberg lace

DIAMONDS *

This pretty design was inspired by the pattern on a paper napkin. The large diamonds can be emphasized with a coloured worker, while the rest of the bobbins are wound with white thread.

BOBBINS: 31 pairs
THREAD: DMC Broder
Machine 50

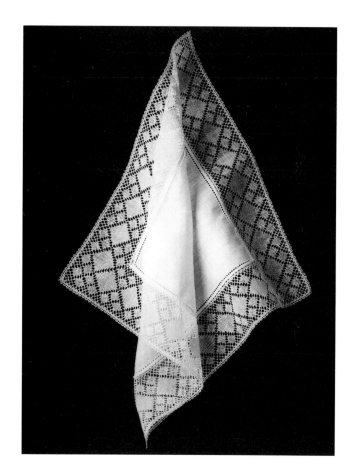

DIAMANTEN *

Grundlage für diesen hübschen Entwurf bildete ein Muster auf einer Papierdecke.
Die großen Diamanten können durch einen farbigen Läufer betont werden, während die restlichen Klöppel mit weißem Garn bewickelt werden.

RUITEN *

Dit leuke ontwerp is geänspireerd op het patroon van een papieren servetje. De grote vierkanten kunnen benadrukt worden door een gekleurd looppaar te gebruiken, terwijl op de rest van de klossen wit garen wordt gewikkeld.

LOSANGE *

Voici un joli dessin inspiré par une nappe en papier. On peut mettre l'accent sur le grand losange en utilisant des voyageurs de couleurs tandis que le reste des fuseaux est bobiné avec du fil blanc.

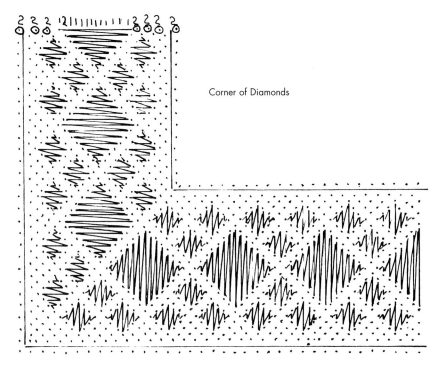

Corner of Diamonds

Corner of Seashore

SEASHORE **

With a torchon shell edge and gimps to represent waves on the shore, this is definitely not difficult. Coloured threads can give an added dimension.

BOBBINS: 25 pairs
 2 single gimps
THREAD: DMC Broder
 Machine 50
 DMC Coton Perlé 5
 for the gimps

MEERESKÜSTE **

Mit einer schmalen Torchon-Muschel-Kante und Konturfäden, die die Wellen am Strand darstellen, ist dieses Muster sicherlich nicht schwicrig. Farbige Fäden können eine weitere Dimension bringen.

ZEEKUST **

Met een Torchonschelp langs de rand en sierdraden om de golven langs het strand weer te geven, is dit beslist niet moeilijk. Gekleurd garen kan een extra dimensie toevoegen.

BORD DE MER **

Faire une bordure Torchon avec des coquilles et des cordons pour faire les vagues, c'est vraiment facile. Les fils couleur peuvent ajouter un plus.

DAISIES **

The unmounted edge shown here is in the style of Beds lace. The slight technical differences are shown in the working diagram. The original piece was made in turquoise.

BOBBINS: 21 pairs
THREAD: DMC Broder
Machine 30

MASSLIEBCHEN **

Die hier gezeigte, nicht montierte Randspitze ist im Stile der Bedford-Spitze gearbeitet. Die leichten technischen Differenzen werden in der Arbeitszeichnung angegeben. Die Originalspitze ist türkis.

MADELIEFJES *

De hier getoonde, niet gemonteerde kant is in de stijl van Bedsfordshire kant. De kleine technische moeilijkheden worden in de werktekening verklaard. De oorspronkelijke kant was in turquoise geklost.

PÂQUERETTES **

Cette bordure qui n'est pas cousue est de style Beds. Les petites différences techniques sont mises en évidence sur le diagramme. La pièce de base est faite en turquoise.

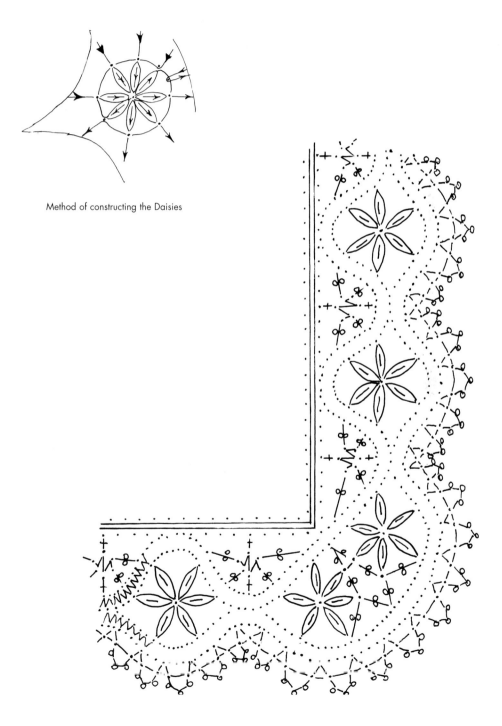

Method of constructing the Daisies

TORCHON EDGE **

Here is an ideal pattern to demonstrate the effectiveness of a variety of torchon stitches. It is not difficult, but the fine thread makes it very delicate.

BOBBINS: 42 pairs
THREAD: BOUC Fil de Lin
140

TORCHON RAND **

Diese Spitze ist ein ideales
Muster, um die Wirksamkeit
verschiedener Torchonschläge
vorzuführen. Sie ist nicht
schwierig, aber das dünne Garn
macht sie sehr reizvoll.

TORCHONRAND **

Dit is een ideaal patroon om het
effect van verschillende
torchonslagen te laten zien. Het is
niet moeilijk, maar door het
dunne garen wordt het een fijn
kantje.

BORDURE TORCHON **

Voilà un modèle idéal pour
mettre en valeur la variété des
points Torchon. Ce n'est pas
difficile, c'est le fil fin qui rend le
travail très délicat.

TORCHON DESIGN ***

Another delicate edge in fine Torchon lace. Here the gimp threads outline the design, and there is scope for the introduction of coloured threads in the shell, trail and gimps.

BOBBINS: 39 pairs
               3 single gimps

THREAD: DMC Broder
              Machine 50
              DMC Coton Perlé 5
              for the gimps

TORCHON DESIGN ***

Eine andere reizvolle Randspitze in feiner Torchonspitze. Hier umrahmen die Konturfäden das Muster und es ist Gelegenheit zur Einführung farbiger Fäden in den Muscheln, dem Streifen und den Konturfäden.

TORCHON ONTWERP ***

Nog een mooie rand in fijne Torchon. Hier omlijnen de sierdraden de tekening, en er is ruimte voor het gebruik van gekleurd garen in de schelpen, de golf en de sierdraden.

MOTIF TORCHON ***

Voici une autre bordure très délicate en fin Torchon. Ici le cordon souligne le dessin et il y a la possibilité d'utiliser les fils couleur pour les coquilles, les rivières et les cordons.

CHAPTER NINE
FLIGHTS OF FANCY

HÖHENFLÜGE DER PHANTASIE ✳ VLUCHT DER
VERBEELDING ✳ BRINS DE FANTAISIE

SERPENTINE *

The Russian tape type of braid commences and finishes in a Bruges scroll. Small beads are sewn on to represent the eyes of the two-headed serpent.

BOBBINS: 8 pairs
             1 pair gimp
THREAD: DMC Special
             Dentelle 80
             DMC Coton Perlé 8
             for gimps
             2 small beads

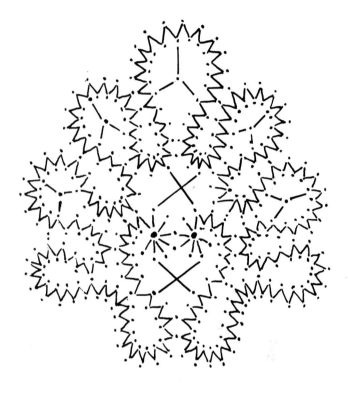

SERPENTINEN *

Das Muster in der Art russischer Bänderspitze beginnt und endet in einem Brügger Krul (vgl. beim „Springbrunnen"). Kleine Perlen werden zur Darstellung der Augen der zweiköpfigen Schlange aufgenäht.

SERPENTINE *

Het ontwerp in de trant van een Russisch bandje begint en eindigt in een Brugse krul. Om de ogen van de tweekoppige slang aan te geven zijn kleine kralen opgenaaid.

SERPENTIN *

Ce type de lacet Russe commence et finit à la façon des volutes de Bruges. On met des perles pour faire les yeux des deux têtes du serpent.

SCHNEEBERG FAN *

This looks very pretty used as a false handkerchief decoration on a top pocket.

BOBBINS: 6 pairs
THREAD: DMC Special
         Dentelle 80

SCHNEEBERGER FÄCHER *

Dies sieht sehr hübsch als
Ziertuchersatz in einer
Brusttasche aus.

SCHNEEBERG WAAIER *

Dit is erg leuk als valse pochette
op de zak van een topje.

EVENTAIL SCHNEEBERG *

Ce sera très joli de l'utiliser en
fausse pochette sur une veste.

LOOPS *

Another free lace design, this has the look and texture of Battenberg lace.

Braid

BOBBINS: 6 pairs
2 pairs gimp
THREAD: DMC Special
Dentelle 80
DMC Coton Perlé 8

Flower

BOBBINS: 6 pairs
THREAD: DMC Special
Dentelle 80

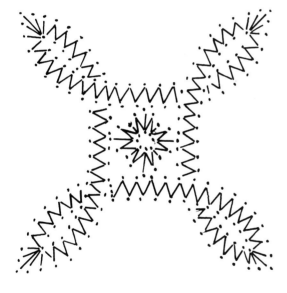

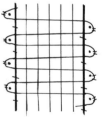

Braid for Loops

ORNAMENT *

Ein Stück in „freier" Spitze mit
geklöppeltem Band – es hat das
Aussehen und die Struktur von
genähter Bändchenspitze (engl.
Battenberg lace).

LUSSEN *

Nog een ontwerp in moderne
kant. Deze keer in de stijl van
Renaissance kant.

BOUCLES *

Voici une autre composition qui a
l'aspect et la texture du Luxeuil.

LILY BUD **

A simple but elegant shape: the flower centre has plaited fillings and the main filling is Dieppe ground, with 2 gimps woven through the filling each side.

BOBBINS: 7 pairs
2 single gimps
THREAD: DMC Special
Dentelle 80
DMC Coton Perlé 8
worked double for
the gimps

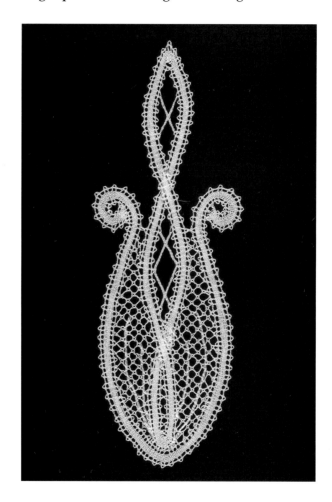

LILIENKNOSPE **

Eine einfache, aber elegante Form: die Blütenmitte hat Flechtenfüllungen und die Hauptfüllung ist Dieppe-Grund. Auf jeder Seite werden 2 Konturfäden durchgewoben.

LELIEKNOP **

Een eenvoudige maar sierlijke vorm: het midden van de bloem heeft een vulling van vlechtjes en de hoofdvulling is Dieppegrond, met aan beide kanten twee sierdraden door de vulling geweven.

BOUTON DE LYS **

De forme simple mais élégante: faire un fond en cordes de 4 au centre et le plus grand fond se fait en point Dieppe avec 2 cordons inclus sur les côtés.

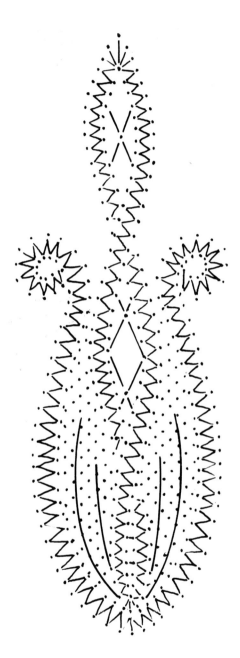

'FLUTTERBY' **

This is worked using Bruges flower lace techniques. Each antenna has a small bead at its tip. To make an antenna, thread 4 pairs through a bead and work in ten-stick to the head, which is worked in whole stitch.

BOBBINS: 6 pairs
THREAD: DMC Special
Dentelle 80
2 small beads

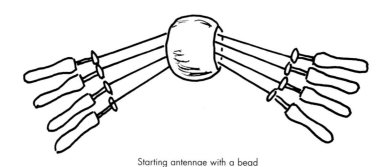

Starting antennae with a bead

"FLUTTERBY" **

Hier werden die Techniken des Brügger Blumenwerks verwendet. Jeder Fühler hat eine kleine Perle an seinem Ende. Für die Antenne werden 4 Fäden durch die Perle gefädelt und es wird eine Rippe bis zum Kopf geklöppelt, der im Leinenschlag folgt.

"FLUTTERBY" **

Deze is volgens de techniek van het Brugs Bloemwerk gemaakt. Iedere voelspriet heeft aan de punt een kraaltje. Om een voelspriet te maken, rijgt u 4 paren door een kraaltje en klost dan een ribje naar de kop, die in linnenslag is gewerkt.

"FLUTTERBY" **

On utilise le Fleuri de Bruges. L'extrémité de chaque antenne est une petite perle. Pour faire l'antenne, accrocher 4 paires sur une perle et faire un lacet contour vers la tête qui sera en toile.

RUSSIAN LACE SAMPLER ***

This design is worked as two simple braids that enclose four areas, in each of which a different traditional Russian tape lace filling is worked.

Outer braid

BOBBINS: 7 pairs
2 pairs gimp
THREAD: DMC Special
Dentelle 80
DMC Coton Perlé 5

Inner braid

BOBBINS: 7 pairs
1 gimp pair

MUSTERTUCH IN
RUSSISCHER
BÄNDERSPITZE ***

Diese Spitze besteht aus zwei
einfachen Bändern, die vier
Bereiche bilden, in denen jeweils
eine andere traditionelle Füllung
russischer Bänder-Spitze
verwendet wird.

SAMPLER IN RUSSISCHE
KANT ***

Dit ontwerp is gewerkt als twee
eenvoudige bandjes, die vier
ruimtes insluiten. In elk hiervan is
een andere traditionele Russische
vulling geklost.

ECHANTILLON EN
RUSSE ***

Ce dessin est fait de deux simples
lacets qui sertissent quatre espaces
dans lesquels sont travaillés
différents fonds traditionnels
Russes.

CHAPTER TEN
ALL-LACE MATS

DECKCHEN ALLER ART ❋ VOLLEDIG KANTEN KLEEDJES ❋

NAPPERON TOUT EN DENTELLE

FLEUR DE LYS *

This design is developed from an original pattern by Daphne Mullen. The corners are rounded and a plait and picot edge added to give a softer outline.

BOBBINS: 11 pairs
THREAD: DMC Broder
Machine 30

FLEUR DE LYS *

Dieses Lilienmuster ist aus einem Originalmuster entwickelt worden von Daphne Mullen. Die Ecken sind abgerundet und ein Flechtenrand mit Pikots hinzugefügt worden, um eine weichere Außenkontur zu bekommen.

FRANSE LELIE *

Dit ontwerp is voortgekomen uit een origineel patroon van Daphne Mullen. De hoeken zijn afgerond en een rand van vlechtjes en picots is toegevoegd voor een vriendelijkere contour.

FLEUR DE LYS *

Ce dessin est fait d'après un modèle de Daphne Mullen. Les coins sont arrondis et on ajoute des bordures en cordes et des picots pour agrémenter l'ensemble.

Fleur de Lys mat

Torchon mat

TORCHON *

Here is a variation of a square mat. It is worked in the same manner as one, but the centre pin along the long side is worked by twisting the ground pair several times round the pin and returning it directly to the work. There is no straight edge and sewings are made at these pins when working up the second long side. The pricking is 80 per cent of the original size.

BOBBINS: 40 pairs
THREAD: BOUC fil de lin 50 (or a finer thread if working to the size illustrated).

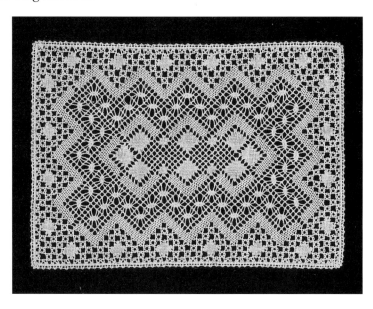

TORCHON *

Dies ist eine Abwandlung einer quadratischen Decke. Sie wurde genauso gearbeitet, aber die Mittelnadel entlang der langen Seite wird geklöppelt, indem das Paar aus dem Grund mehrere Male um die Nadel gedreht wird und direkt weiterarbeitet. Es gibt keine gerade Kante und an diesen Nadeln muß eingehäkelt werden, wenn die zweite Seite geklöppelt wird. Der Klöppelbrief hat 80 % der Originalgröße.

TORCHON *

Dit is een variatie op een vierkant kleed. Het is op dezelfde manier gewerkt als een vierkant kleed, maar op de middenspeld aan de lange zijde wordt het paar uit de grond een paar maal gedraaid, waarna het direct weer in het werk teruggaat. Daar is geen rechte rand en bij het klossen van de tweede lange zijde wordt op deze spelden aangehaakt. De prikking is op 80% van de oorspronkelijke grootte.

TORCHON *

Voici une variation d'un napperon carré. Il se fait de la même façon, mais l'épingle centrale sur le grand côté se travaille avec les passives du fond qu'on tourne plusieurs fois autour de l'épingle avant qu'elles ne retournent à leur travail. Il n'y a pas de bord droit et on fait des accrochages sur ces épingles quand on fait le deuxième grand côté. Ce modèle est à 80% de la taille réelle.

OVAL SCHNEEBERG **

The edge design is worked in Schneeberg techniques, using 4 pairs of passives instead of the more usual 3 pairs. The centre filling is a plaited one.

BOBBINS: 7 pairs
THREAD: BOUC fil de lin 80

OVALES SCHNEEBERGER **

Das Muster am Rande ist in Schneeberger Technik geklöppelt. Verwendet wurden 4 statt der gebräuchlicheren 3 Rißpaare. Die Mitte erhält eine Flechterfüllung.

OVAAL SCHNEEBERG **

De rand is in Schneebergtechniek geklost, met 4 hangende paren in plaats van de meer gebruikelijke 3. De middenvulling bestaat uit vlechtjes.

OVAL EN SCHNEEBERG **

La bordure se fait en Schneeberg, on utilise 4 paires passives en lieu des 3 traditionnelles. On fait un fond en corde de 4 au centre

Oval Schneeberg mat

Round Beds mat

ROUND BEDS **

Adapted from an original design by Kathleen Hillyer, this pretty mat is worked in Beds lace.

BOBBINS: 33 pairs
THREAD: DMC Broder
Machine 30

RUNDES BEDFORD **

Dieses schöne Deckchen, abgewandelt von einem Originalentwurf von Kathleen Hillyer, wird in Bedford-Spitze geklöppelt.

ROND KLEED IN BEDSFORDSHIRE KANT **

Dit mooie kleed, een variatie op een origineel ontwerp van Kathleen Hillyer, is gewerkt als Bedsfordshire kant.

ROND EN BEDS **

Adapté d'un dessin original de Kathleen Hillyer, ce joli napperon se fait en Beds.

SQUARE ***

This pricking is neither quick nor easy, but a challenge. Worked mainly in half-stitch, the design was inspired by a knitted lace mat. The corner leaves are worked in half-stitch with the same worker, beginning at the base of the first leaf and finishing at the base of the fourth.

BOBBINS: 41 pairs
THREAD: BOUC fil de lin 50

QUADRAT ***

Dieser Klöppelbrief ist weder schnell noch leicht, aber eine Herausforderung. Dieser Spitze, hauptsächlich im Halbschlag geklöppelt, diente ein gestricktes Deckchen als Vorlage. Die Blätter an den Ecken sind im Halbschlag mit demselben Laufpaar gearbeitet. Man fängt an der Basis des ersten Blattes an und endet an der Basis des vierten Blattes.

VIERKANT ***

Deze prikking is noch snel noch gemakkelijk, maar een uitdaging. Het voornamelijk in netslag gekloste ontwerp is geānspireerd op een gebreid kleed. De bladeren op de hoeken zijn in netslag geklost met dezelfde loper, beginnend aan de basis van het eerste blad en eindigend aan de basis van het vierde.

CARRÉ ***

Voici un modèle qui n'est ni rapide, ni simple mais un vrai défi. Il se fait surtout en grille, le dessin est inspiré d'un napperon en tricot d'Art. Les feuilles dans les angles se font en grille en utilisant les mêmes voyageurs et commençant à la base de la première pour finir à la base de la quatrième.

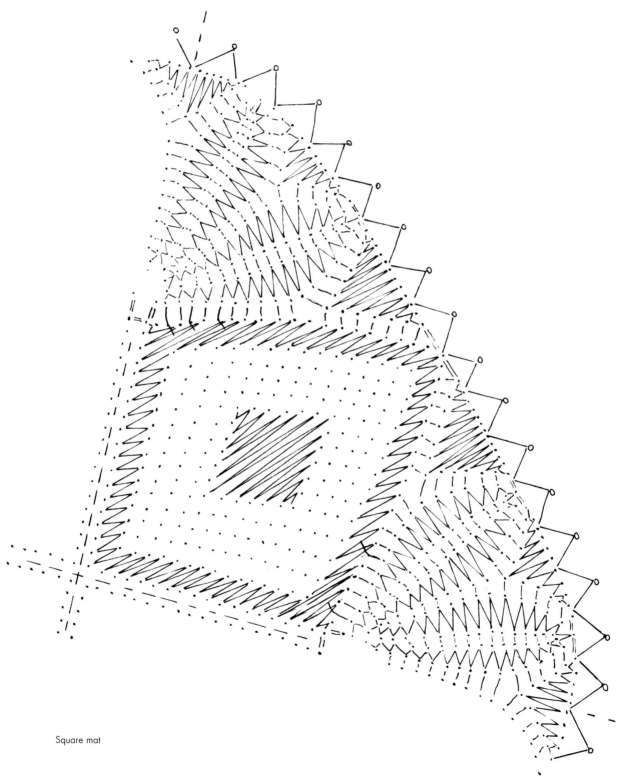

Square mat

ESSENTIAL READING

Baumeister-Jonker, Lia. *Schneeberger Lace*, issued by Springetts

Cook, Bridget. *Practical Skills in Bobbin Lace*, B.T. Batsford

Cook, Bridget. *Russian Tape Lace*, B.T. Batsford

Karpenko, Tatiana and Aleksai. *Grounds for Russian Lace*, Lebenshilfe Leer e.V.

Luxton, Elsie. *The Technique of Honiton Lace*, B.T. Batsford

Nottingham, Pamela. *The Technique of Torchon Lace*, B.T. Batsford

Nottingham, Pamela. *Bedfordshire Lace Making*, B.T. Batsford

Nottingham, Pamela. *The Techniques of Bobbin Lace*, B.T. Batsford

van Olffen-Spikermann, Annelie. *Schneeberger Kant*, Cantecleer

Polfliet-Pauwels, M. *Russische Kant*, Terra

Rombach-de Kievid, J. *Bruges Bloemwerk*, Terra

Sorenson, Veronica. *Modern Lace Designs*, B.T. Batsford

Sorenson, Veronica. *Design Techniques for Modern Lace*, B.T. Batsford

Sorenson, Veronica and de Kievid, J. Rombach. *The Technique of Bruges Flower Lace*, B.T. Batsford

Stott, G. and Cook, B. *Book of Bobbin Lace Stitches*, B.T. Batsford

Thompson, Susanne. *Introduction to Honiton Lace*, B.T. Batsford

LIST OF SUPPLIERS

UK

A.R. Archer (bobbins)
Yew Tree Cottage
High Street
Walsham Le Willows
Bury St Edmunds

Arthur Sells
49 Pedley Lane
Clifton
Shefford SG17 5QT

Barleycroft Lacemaking
Supplies, 'Honeypuddle'
13 Barleycroft
Stevenage SG2 9NP

Evelyn and Tony Brown
(Pillow makers)
Temple Lane Cottage
Littledean
GL14 3NX

Bryncraft Bobbins
B.J. Phillips
Pantglas
Cellan
Lampeter
Dyfed SA48 8JD

Doreen Campbell
(frames and mounts)
Highcliff
Bremilham Road
Malmesbury SN16 0DQ

Jo Firth
Lace Making & Needlecraft
Supplies
58 Kent Crescent
Lowtown
Pudsey LS28 9EB

John & Jennifer Ford
(mail order, and lace
days only)
October Hill
Upper Longdon
Rugeley WS15 1QB

Framecraft Miniatures Ltd
372-376 Summer Lane
Hockley
Birmingham B19 3QA

D.J. Hornsby
25 Manwood Avenue
Canterbury CT2 7AH

Mainly Lace
Moulsham Mill
Parkway
Chelmsford
Essex CM2 7PX

T. Parker (mail order,
general supplies and
bobbins)
124 Corhampton Road
Boscombe East
Bournemouth BH6 5NZ

Stephen Pearce
Yew Tree Cottage
Chapel Road
Grundisburgh
Woodbridge IP13 6TS

Piper Silks
(specialist silk yarns)
'Chinnery's'
Egremont Street
Glemsford
CO10 7SA

Peter & Beverley Scarlett
Strupak
Hill Head
Cold Wells, Ellon
Grampion

J.S. Sear
Lacecraft Supplies
8 Hillview
Sherington MK16 9NJ

Sebalace
Waterloo Mill
Howden Road
Silsden BD20 0HA

SMP Lace
The Lace Workshop
1 Blays, Churchfield Road
Chalfont St Peter SL9 0HB

Spangles, The Bead People
Carole Morris
1 Casburn Lane
Burwell CB5 0ED

Christine & David
Springett
21 Hillmorton Road
Rugby CV22 5DF

Stitches and Lace
Alby Craft Centre
Cromer Road
Alby
Norwich NR11 7QE

Winslow Bobbins
70 Magpie Way
Winslow MK18 3PZ

GERMANY

Barbara Fay Verlag &
Versandbuchhandlung
Am Goosberg 2
D-24340 Gammelby

Rittersgrüner
Klöppelboutique
Barbara Neubert
Karlsbader Str. 43
D-08355 Rittersgrün

THE NETHERLANDS

Theo Brejaart
Dordstelaan 146
P.O. Box 5199
3008 AD Rotterdam

Heikina de Rüyter
Zuiderstraat 1
9693 ER Nieuweschans

Magazijn *De Vlijt*
Lijnmarkt 48
3511 KJ Utrecht

FRANCE

La Galerie
Centre d'Enseignement à
la Dentelle Au Fuseau
1 Rue Raphaël
43000 Le Puy en Velay

A L'Econome
Anne-Marie Deydier
Ecole de Dentelle aux
Fuseaux
10 rue Paul Chenavard
69001 Lyon

INDEX